The Chronicles of RUTH

Blogging Through My 80s

Ruth Baird Shaw

Ruth Shaw remembers a time when folks sat in rocking chairs on the front porch and shared stories. Today, at age 88, she sits at her computer and shares those memories with people all over the world.

Dedication

The Chronicles of Ruth is dedicated to my daughters, Joan Shaw Turrentine and Carol Shaw Johnston, who helped me start blogging by setting up my weblog, **Ruthlace** (http://ruthlace.blogspot.com). Without their talent and priceless help, neither the blog nor this book would have seen the light of day.

Copyright October 2011
Ruth Baird Shaw

Ruth Baird Shaw
Proverbs 3 : 5 - 6

ISBN 978-0-557-83002-2
90000

9 780557 830022

Acknowledgments

My deep appreciation goes to my daughter, Carol Shaw Johnston, for the editing and formatting of *The Chronicles of Ruth* and to my daughter, Joan Shaw Turrentine, for putting the best of my blog posts into book form, from which this book was started. Their valuable help and computer expertise made the publishing of this work possible.

My love and appreciation go to my family, many of whom, at one time or another, were available to teach me all I know about the computer as well as the Internet.

I bought a computer in 1987 and was thrilled that it made correcting my slow typing less troublesome. The word processing is still a joy for me.

The Chronicles of Ruth was begun for my children, the loves of my life: Janice, Joan, Terrell, Carol, Deborah, Beth and David. It is also for my precious daughters-in-law, Sheila and Vicki; my dear sons-in-law, Gilbert, Jim, Ron, Gregg and Chuck; and for my 18 grandchildren and to my 18 great-grandchildren. The names of all are included on page 254.

The Chronicles of Ruth is in loving memory of my husband, Charles Columbus Shaw; my parents, Benjamin Wilson Baird and Ieula Ann Dick Baird; and my eight siblings: Wilson Grice Baird, William Bogan (Willie B.) Baird, Louise Baird McCullough Lee Campbell, Vera Baird Loyd, Mary Elizabeth Baird Shepherd, Charles (Charlie) Morrison Baird, John Thomas Baird, Jackson Irvin Baird and for their children and future descendants.

Introduction

The Chronicles of Ruth began in 2005 as my blog, **Ruthlace** (http://ruthlace.blogspot.com). I started blogging with the help of my daughters, Carol and Joan. Joan's suggestion of "Ruthlace" as the weblog name rang a bell with me. Soon, **Ruthlace** was off and running.

I began **Ruthlace** to tell family history and stories for my children, for extended family and for other descendants of my parents. I was encouraged to keep writing as Weblog Awards readers kept choosing **Ruthlace** as one of the finalists in the Best Diarist category every year from 2006 forward.

Feedback from many people tells me they read and relate to the stories of my life experiences in the 1920s and 1930s as well as my poems and the observations of modern life.

I write about the boll weevil destruction that took King Cotton off the throne of America's Southland. I write about my father's difficult decision in 1922 to give up his life as a farmer to find work in a nearby textile town to support his still growing family. A few of the incidents I write about are told in more than one story so that each post can stand alone.

The Great Depression stories and accounts of life before, during and after World War II on **Ruthlace** are about everything from "Fresh off the Farm," "Bed and Bath in the 1920s and 1930s" and "A Glimpse of Romance during World War II" to "One Sunday Morning" and "Pioneer Clergywomen" much later in my life.

Some of my posts on **Ruthlace** tell stories learned from my mother. "School in the Southland in the 1890s" is a fact filled story related to me by my mother who was born March 6, 1885 and started to school in a one-room schoolhouse in 1891.

One popular post is about my childhood memory of seeing my first parade. It was a "Civil War Parade" featuring the last of the disappearing Confederate soldiers of the Civil War. It is a reminder of today's (2011) news releases telling of the "disappearing World War II soldiers." I also write about my experience as a Caucasian growing up in the segregated South.

At the suggestion of my family and friends, I am including some of my poems published in my 2010 book *Life with Wings* as well as life experiences and happenings since World War II.

I have loved to write since early childhood when I tried to compose poems with a lead pencil on lined tablets and scraps of paper. At age 88, I continue writing but (beyond my wildest dreams as a child) I now write on a computer to a worldwide Internet audience. A brief look at my blog's site meter recently indicates that people from over 100 different countries have checked *Ruthlace* during the months of June and July.

I trust those who read *The Chronicles of Ruth* will enjoy the reading as much as I have enjoyed the writing.

Ruth Baird Shaw
October 2011

Contents

Historical

Stories from the 1890s through World War II

Charles and Ruth Shaw during World War II

Fresh off the Farm

Mama always said the boll weevil ran us off the farm.[1] Cotton was king in the South. When the destructive cotton boll weevil ate its way east through Mississippi and Alabama into Georgia in 1919, it infested the cotton plants and wiped out cotton as the major money crop. My father, along with other Georgia farmers, lost his beautiful white fields of cotton and thus his whole year's wages.

My father, Wilson Baird, was in failing health when he finally got a job in one of the three textile factories in Porterdale and moved his family "fresh off the farm" into that "model mill town" in the fall of 1922. I was born the next year.

My older cousin, Aubrey Simms, told me a few years before he died in the 1990s that he remembered as a boy of nine, the very night in 1922 when my father told his father, Jason Simms, of his decision to give up his farm and get a job in the nearby textile village. His father replied, "Uncle Wilson, I will go to share-cropping before I will raise my children in a mill town."

Apparently, my father believed he had no other option. I am told my father worked as long as he was able in the Old Porterdale Mill located on the Yellow River. He died in 1932 after being bedridden for nearly a year.

The textile industry had moved south in the early 1900s for less expensive labor and found plenty of people needing jobs among the white and African American people in the Civil War torn southland part of the United States.[2]

Two of my brothers, John Thomas (Tom) Baird and Jackson Irvin (Jack) Baird, spoke so highly and longed so fervently to get back to

---

[1] The farm was in the community of Oak Hill in Newton County near the Henry
[2] Bibb Manufacturing Company built the three large factory buildings, all the housing for employees, the schools, businesses, and churches – the whole town. There was a community doctor, nurse and social worker. Someone told me recently that the mill village system was patterned after the plantation system.

their hometown when they were serving during World War II, many of their World War II buddies vowed they would one day visit Porterdale.

Happy memories of Porterdale and nostalgia for the community spirit and interest continue to this day with a Porterdale Reunion in August every year.

Tom served in the Army Infantry in Europe. Jack served in the Air Force in the South Pacific. My brothers came home after the war. Sadly, many soldiers did not. Carroll Adams, Quinton "Red" Cole, James Homer Cook, and J.W. Rye, my friends and classmates, were among those who did not survive to come back home from World War II.

After World War II, and the advent of labor laws in the mid to late 1940's, much of the industry closed down most of their "looms and twisters" in Georgia and moved farther South outside the United States. With no jobs in their hometown, my brothers and others had to look elsewhere.

My brother, Tom Baird, worked briefly as a policeman in Porterdale after WW II and later was a State Patrol trooper. Tom lived with his family in Cedartown, Georgia as a Sergeant in the Georgia State Patrol until his death in 1998.

My youngest brother, Jack Baird, worked as short-order cook in a restaurant in Savannah for a time, as a pipe-fitter and later as the supervisor of pipe-fitters at large mall construction sites in South Carolina until his death in 1989.

However, my brothers and schoolmates thought, and so do I, that Porterdale was a great place to grow up in the 1920s and 1930s. Our school teachers and community leaders were the best. [3]

---

[3] My teachers in Porterdale School were: First Grade – Miss Jones, Second Grade – Miss Wright, Third Grade – Miss Web, 4th Grade – Mrs. Tommie Hood, 5th Grade – Miss Bura Bohanan, 6th Grade – Mrs. Pearl Hacket, 7th Grade – Miss Willie Hayne Hunt, 8th Grade – Mr. John F. Allumns, 9th Grade – Mrs. Willie Hayne Hunt. Miss Ethel Belcher was principal of the school when I started

The two large red brick Porterdale School buildings had classrooms for first grade through grade nine. There was also a music room and a home economics classroom with sewing machine and stove and refrigerator.

Adjacent to one of the school buildings was a large, "state of the art" indoor swimming pool. One of my earliest memories is learning to swim in the enclosed pool. A few years later the brick building that surrounded the pool was removed and we enjoyed the outdoor swimming pool.

The ninth grade was the last grade in the Porterdale School System in the late thirties. One had to pay tuition and find transportation to Covington (our county seat) or to one of the rural high schools to graduate from high school. However, with little money and few cars this was difficult.

Our neighbors were very much a part of my life as a child. I have fond memories of being in and out of the homes of the Finchers, the Parnells, the Hornings and the Moores. And they visited with us daily. We did not lock our doors - even at night. Neighbors were in and out all the time - often to borrow a cup of sugar or flour or an egg or two to finish out a recipe. Often neighbors stopped in to share vegetables or cookies. [4]

In those financially difficult times, many people lived from paycheck to paycheck. Mama seemed to always have an extra dollar or two to loan to anyone who ran out of cash before the next payday.

---

school. Miss Maud King was principal when I finished at Porterdale and started to Covington High School.

[4] Hazel Street playmates included Dorothy, Hazel and Lamar Fincher, Mamie Miller, E. F. Parnell, Obie and Billie Moore, Hazel and Sybil Horning, Jeanette and Betty Martin. Other Hazel Street friends were Julia Sellers, Mildred Yancey and Frank Ingram. I kept in touch with Julia Sellers Smith until her death in 2000, but have not heard from most of the other in many years. I think of them often and would like to hear from them and their family and friends.

Our house was often the gathering place where neighbors would gather to sit on the swing and the big porch rocking chairs or on the steps after all the chairs were filled.

With no television or telephone and few radios, sometimes the visits lasted late into the evening; the adults resting on the front porch after a hard day's work and talking together while the children played "hide and seek" or "kick the can" out in the front yard or on the unpaved road in front of the house.

Going to School in the 1930s

I started school in January before my sixth birthday in 1929. This was the year of the stock market crash and the Great Depression. I

suppose we had "poverty" but not in the sense of poverty today. Most people were in the same boat and helped one another. We were fortunate not to have 24 hour news, so we did not learn until later that people were jumping out of skyscraper windows to kill themselves.

The first five grades in our school were divided into 10 grades. We had low first grade and high first, low second, high second, etc. I contracted measles and missed the last two weeks of school in the low fifth grade.

When my teacher came by to visit a few days after school was out for the summer she brought my report card. Yes, teachers, doctors and pastors were expected to make house calls! Mama asked my teacher if I was to go back in the fifth grade or skip to the sixth grade. She gave me a test and skipped me to the sixth grade. That is how I happened to be the youngest in my class for the rest of my elementary and high school. Elementary school was called "grammar school" back then.

School dress: In grammar school in those days, girls always wore dresses to school with knee stockings and oxford-type shoes or high top shoes. I remember a few of the girls wore high-top stockings. These were dark, thick stockings - often black - that came above the knee and were held secure by elastic circles. In fact these garters were called "elastics." We had only one pair of shoes that were usually worn until they fell apart. I have worn shoes that had cardboard inserted to cover holes in the soles of the shoe. I remember being thankful that my mother did not make me wear those "old fashioned stockings."

Incidentally, a little later when we did wear sheer hose with a seam down the center of the back that had to be kept straight, we made our own elastics to keep our hosiery up. We just took a piece of elastic and measured around the leg just above the knee and sewed the ends of the elastic together. This was before garter belts were in use. By the time I got to high school, girls were beginning to wear anklets that turned down at the ankle and so were more comfortable.

Discipline: As I was writing this, a longtime friend called. When he learned I was writing about school in the 1930s, he asked if I had written about "whippings." I told him that "whippings were a "boy thing." After we joked around a bit, we both agreed that in his school in South Carolina and mine in Georgia, the teachers had twelve-inch rulers that were used for something besides measuring distance. The disobedient child held his/her hand out with palm up to be smacked with a ruler. For major misbehavior, a razor strop or a hickory switch was used on the child's bottom. Parents typically told children that if they "got a whipping" at school, they would "get another one" at home. Litigation against teachers and/or schools was not considered.

School Room: The student desks were attached to one another in rows. They were also attached to the floor. All student desks faced the large teacher's desk. The wall behind the teacher desk was covered with blackboards for writing. The blackboards had narrow little shelves at the bottom to hold chalk and erasers. Each of the student desktops had a small round hole that our ink wells fit into. We had to fill our pens with ink from the ink wells for writing before fountain pens came on the market. We also used pencils and lined tablets for math, spelling and much of our writing. Every week, two students were selected to take the erasers outside to "dust the erasers" to get all the chalk dust out so they would be clean enough to keep the blackboard clean for clear writing.

Social Class: The word egalitarian had never been spoken! I remember clearly sitting in class while the teacher told us there were three classes of people: the upper, the middle and the lower class. We did not, for the most part, question this custom. Socially, people associated with their own class as well as their own race.

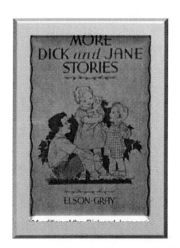

Transportation: How did we get to school? Two words. We walked! In our school, most of the teachers also walked. Many were single women who lived in town. In our town we had a large house called the "teacher's cottage." The teachers' house was across the river from the school building. There were no parking lots at the schoolhouse.

Report Cards: In our small-town Georgia school, we were graded A, B, C, D or F. I do not remember anything about the grading system or how I scored in first and second grades. I do know that I never received a D or an F and do not remember many As. I was generally a B student. I usually sat quietly and went unnoticed in class, speaking only when spoken to.

Miscellaneous Thoughts: We were then taught that the atom was the smallest particle. It was not until 1945 that we learned that that microscopic atom could be split and inside was power beyond comprehension.

Ruth Baird Shaw

One of my readers asked about "school dinners." There was not a cafeteria in the elementary school I attended or the high schools I attended. However, there was a home economics class where all the girls took lessons in homemaking; basically in cooking and sewing.

In our "Grammar School", we could "take milk" for three cents a day. It consisted of a small bottle of milk and a sandwich of peanut butter spread on two very thin slices of white bread. Most of the children brought a lunch from home, typically a biscuit with sausage or fried meat or jelly.

The group picture above is my ninth grade graduation class. The ninth grade was the last grade offered in our community in the 1930s. It wasn't until the 1940s that Porterdale High School was established. Yours truly (Ruth Baird) was fourth girl on the left, front row.

After ninth grade graduation, students who desired to finish tenth grade and eleventh grade and receive a high school diploma had to pay tuition, buy their books and find transportation to Covington, our Newton County seat. Ninth Grade was the end of school for many students in the thirties.

I ended up attending three different high schools. My widowed mother somehow managed the tuition cost for me to attend Covington High School and another small transportation fee to a girl in my class who had managed to buy a car. I rode with her (Louise Walton) to Covington every school day for a full semester. Alas, she dropped out or decided not to continue in school. Perhaps high school students then, as now, may have spent more time with their cars than their books!

Pictured above, left to right, in 1943: Ruth Baird Shaw, Clara Shaw Daniel, Lenora Mills, Gladys Newnan

With no transportation to Covington after the first semester in the tenth grade, I then transferred to Livingston High School, a county high school. I walked with 2 other girls and a boy (Julia Sellers, Hilda Mitchell, Ernest Bennett) the mile or so every morning to the far end of our community to catch the school bus to ride to the county school where I finished the tenth grade with only two units left to graduate. In the 1930s, students received a high school diploma after finishing the eleventh grade.

Porterdale established a high school in 1940. Older students were allowed to attend, so my husband went back to classes and graduated in 1942 and I in 1943. When I finally managed to enroll in college classes, I learned my high school experiences had been well enough preparation.

One of the things I remember about Covington High School in the semester I attended was an assignment to write a story of fiction. As far back as I remember, I have loved to write and enjoyed writing rhymes. I remember working on the story but do not remember anything about it. As I remember, it was basically a lazy rearrangement of something I had read - which is probably why I do not remember anything about the story. When we take shortcuts or cheat on anything, we only cheat ourselves. Strangely, I have never taken time to try to write fiction again.

Another day, while I was a student at Covington High, we went to Chapel where someone introduced a blind and deaf lady and illustrated how she communicated. This memory is too vague for me to be sure of details. I keep thinking it must have been Helen Keller and her teacher? Did Keller and her teacher visit high schools in Georgia in 1938? Who else could it be? I believe that the famed Annie Sullivan, Helen's first teacher, died in 1936. Polly Thomson assisted Sullivan later and became Helen's teacher after Annie Sullivan's death.

I've told about an earlier chapel experience in the first or second grade when I was chosen to walk up on the large stage in the grammar school auditorium to tell the Bible story of the sick man whose four friends took him, bed and all, to Jesus to be healed.

Teachers: I especially remember one of the teachers at Livingston High School, the school where I transferred after my friend with a car left Covington High. One unforgettable teacher at Livingston was a widow in perpetual black dress. She was always openly counting the days until the end of the school year. I do not know how long she had been a widow, but this thin and sad looking lady in her "widow's weeds" each day would tell us how she was counting the days until the end of her days as a teacher. Then she would remind us how many days were left in the school year. She called herself the "walking calendar."

Another teacher I remember more fondly was Miss Willie Hayne Hunt, my seventh grade teacher in Porterdale. She tried to encourage me by telling me I was probably the "best mathematician that ever walked in the school door." This kind of remark from a teacher made a big difference in the way I saw myself as a student. I began to find algebra and geometry problems not just easy but fun to do.

Cooking From Scratch

When one "cooked from scratch" in the 1920s and 1930s, it was from the first "scratch" of a match. We had a large iron cook stove in our kitchen when I was a child. The iron cook stove burned wood.

Wood had to be cut in "stove wood" lengths, brought from the backyard into the house and stacked in wood boxes behind the stove. A fire had to be started with crumpled up newspaper and kindling wood. Then the fire was kept burning by the constant addition of larger pieces of stove wood.

This stove looks much like the stove in our kitchen in the late 1920s and early 1930s except our stove had white metal on the oven door and warming closets.

The stove had what we called "a warming closet" near the top. It had two decorative iron doors to open and place cooked food to keep warm until time to set on the table.

A large reservoir was built in on the side to heat water. I remember one of my jobs was to keep water in the reservoir. The "eyes" on top of the stove could be removed to build the fire. There was a little iron utensil to fit into a hole in the stove eye to lift it and then put back in place so large pots of beans or potatoes or meat could be cooked on top of the stove. I remember my mother cooking beef roast, pork roast, and chickens on top of the stove in water. We called them "roasts", but they were sometimes boiled or simmered on top of the stove. This was used possibly for tougher cuts of meat than the roasts we cook today.

Chicken, pork chops, and cubed steak was fried in a large iron skillet. I have seen my mother use a hammer to pound steak to tenderize it. She would then flour and fry it in serving size pieces. Meat was not served every day.

Some kind of dried beans (a wonderful source of protein) was cooked almost every day - large butter beans, small limas, pinto beans, navy beans, or black-eyed peas. Salt pork was plentiful and added to the dried vegetables for seasoning. Potatoes were boiled with butter and sometimes dumplings - probably bits of leftover dough from the biscuits that were cooked at every meal. The term "low-fat" had never been spoken!

Large pans of sweet potatoes were baked often. Sweet potatoes seemed plentiful and were sometimes fried or made into pies or puddings. In the summer, fresh vegetables were cooked in place of or in addition to the dried beans which were a staple and inexpensive source of protein nearly every day. Fresh vegetables were seasoned with fat meat (uncured bacon). Thankfully my mother did not add the fat meat to fresh vegetables as lavishly as some cooks did.

My favorite summer vegetable plate was fresh crowder peas with a few tiny pods of okra boiled on top of the peas, fresh corn cut finely off the cob, and sliced tomatoes. On a cold winter day nothing was better than chicken and dumplings, one of Mama's really great dishes. What kind of bread? We had cornbread, of course, and hot buttered biscuits.

Mama made great vegetable soup from fresh tomatoes and an assortment of vegetables from summer gardens. She also made soup in the winter using canned tomatoes and canned corned beef with potatoes, rice, or macaroni and any vegetables she had. We had canned salmon made into patties fairly often and sometimes fried fish. The fish meal was often fish that Mama caught from the nearby Yellow River.

Cheese and macaroni, rice, and rice pudding were common dishes in the 30s. Grits and eggs were often served for breakfast with fried salt pork or streak-o-lean. Sometimes we had ham to go along with biscuits with butter and jelly or jam that had been prepared and put away in jars in quantity during the summer. It was not uncommon to have pork chops or fried chicken for breakfast along with the regular homemade buttered biscuits with real butter.

The first margarine I saw looked like a hunk of lard, and, for a long time, tasted like lard to me - as it did to anyone who had been raised on country-buttered biscuits. The margarine of the late thirties was white and came with a vial of yellow coloring. To make it look more like butter, the margarine had to be left out of the refrigerator to soften at room temperature. The yellow coloring had to be worked in. I suppose the butter lobbyists mandated this. In a few years the margarine people prevailed and they were allowed to make margarine that looked as yellow as butter.

An after-dinner speaker named Baldy White was popular when I was young. He was a big man and used to keep his audience laughing with such comments as, "We were so poor when I was a boy; all we had for breakfast was ham, eggs, buttered grits and hot biscuits with an assortment of homemade jellies and preserves. We didn't know there was such a thing as Post Toasties!"

I remember Aunt Cora bringing her two granddaughters my age, Mildred and Allene, down from their home in Atlanta one week-end and how excited they were to have homemade biscuits for breakfast. I was amazed. I would have been more excited to have cereal and milk or toast made with "store bought" bread. Rare!

School in the Southland in the 1890s

My mother was only 18 months old when her father, Charles Dick, died - leaving a pregnant wife and seven little children. As a child, Ieula Ann Dick never knew her paternal relatives, but she was told her Grandfather Dick had been the first sheriff of Clay County, Alabama. I am told her Grandfather Dick's picture is still on the wall of the Clay County Courthouse.

Mama's young father had gone hunting late on a cold Christmas Day. He became ill with a cold that turned into pneumonia which proved fatal. Sometime after her father's untimely death, Mama's maternal grandfather, Bogan Mask, moved his daughter, Elizabeth, and her children from Alabama to a small house on his large farm in Inman, Georgia. Inman was a farming community in Fayette County, Georgia. It was there that the grieving widow, Elizabeth, gave birth to her eighth child, a son.

I do not know how Charles Dick in Clay County, Alabama met Elisabeth Mask in Inman, Georgia, but apparently Bogan Mask thought Charles Dick worthy to marry his oldest daughter.

Mama loved her Grandfather Mask who tried to be a father to his oldest daughter's fatherless children. He was hard-working and prosperous for the times - a farmer and a Methodist preacher.

Aunt Cora, my mother's older sister, thought Elizabeth and her eight little children were often overlooked by their prosperous relatives. However, Mama said her mother was aware of her dependence and was timid about informing her father of their needs.

Mama grew up to marry Wilson Baird when she was 18 years old. He was 40. Wilson was the youngest son of William and Mary Baird. William had served as an officer in the Confederate Army and was wounded in the Battle of the Wilderness. His older sister's husband had been killed while serving in the Confederate Army, leaving his wife with a child to rear. Papa stayed on the farm to help his mother and widowed sister raise his niece, and so waited until the age of 40 to marry.

I am the youngest of Wilson and Ieula's eleven children - nine of whom survived into adulthood.

Mama told me a little about the school she attended. As was typical in the South, this bright little girl went to school only too briefly in the war-ravaged South where many of the schools and houses had been torched as General Sherman and his Army moved through the Southland "all the way to the sea."

Mama told me about Professor Culpepper who taught her through all the arithmetic books and into much of algebra in the little one room schoolhouse near Inman before, all too soon, she had to leave school to work in the fields and on the farm.

My cousin, S.J. Overstreet, sent me this picture of the one-room Inman Schoolhouse in Fayette County, Georgia. Professor Culpepper is shown on the back row.

School was a luxury few in the South could afford. When I asked Mama what grade she completed, she told me they did not have grade levels in the1890s as we then had in the early 1930s. However, her formal education was probably somewhat equal to a ninth grade education. Sadly, this was more formal education than many of the women in our neighborhood had during the Great Depression years (late 1920s-1930s)

Mama revered Professor Culpepper, and told me how he took time to teach algebra to her in that one room schoolhouse. Mama was also glad to tell me that, in a world divided by class as well as race and gender, her father and her mother's family "came from good stock." They valued education for the girls as well as the boys.

When I think of how valuable family history is to us today, I know the need for all of America's children to hear the unique history of America at a time of worldwide illiteracy, slavery, class and racial divisions.

Thankfully, we did overcome many of these problems. It is sad when we spend our time down the road to bitterness and political division of class and ethnicity and the destruction of our hard won life, liberty and the pursuit of happiness.

Taffy Pulls and Tea Cakes in the 1920s and 30s

In my childhood, we sometimes got together with the neighbors and made taffy or "pull candy" at our house.

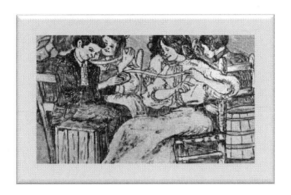

Recipe for Old Fashioned Taffy (Pull Candy)

2 cups sugar
½ cup vinegar
½ cup water
2 Tablespoon butter

Bring to a boil, cooking until mixture will spin a long thread (or to 275 degrees on a candy thermometer). Remove from heat, add 1 teaspoon vanilla and pour into greased plates until cool enough to handle. When the candy begins to "set", wash and butter your hands, take a little ball of the hot candy (about the size of a small egg), and pull and twist it, or possibly plait it, until it begins to get cool and hard. Then place it on a buttered plate and cut into sticks of candy.

Often Mama made tea cakes -- thick, chewy cookies cut out with a biscuit cutter or tea glass. As a special treat she would make a chocolate fudge frosting (made from scratch, of course) and put two cookies together with the chocolate between.

These cookies she stored in a washed flour sack. Aluminum foil and plastic wrap were not available at the market in those days.

Mama baked tea cakes often for children, grandchildren and the neighbors' children. These tea cakes were sometimes brought out and served to neighbors as we visited on the front porch. Our house was usually the visiting place. The younger couples, whose oldest children were near my age, seemed to love to congregate on our porch and visit.

Recipe for Mama's Tea Cakes

1 cup shortening	½ cup milk
2 cups sugar	1 tsp. vanilla
2 eggs	2 cups self-rising flour

Mix all ingredients together.
Add enough flour to make a stiff ball of dough,
Roll out thin.
Cut with cookie cutters and put on a cookie sheet.
Bake at 400 until brown, about 8 to 15 minutes.

Ruth Baird Shaw

Washing Clothes in Tubs with Rub Boards

Monday was "Wash Day" in my childhood in the late 1920s and early 30s. Wash Day was a long day. The family's clothes were washed weekly in large galvanized tin tubs. Soapy hot water was prepared in one tub, and rinse water in two other tubs. A rub board was put in the wash tub, and clothes were scrubbed on the rub board.

A big cast iron pot was set up on bricks out in the back yard, and a fire was built under it to heat the water and to boil the clothes. This was done winter and summer every week. Talk about a hard day's work!

The clean clothes were pinned with wooden clothespins to a long wire or rope clothesline to, hopefully, dry in the sun. On cold winter days, the clothes would sometimes freeze as fast as they were pinned to the line. Our wet hands would turn purple before all the clothes were hung up to dry.

Hopefully the sun and wind would dry the laundered clothes enough to be brought inside before dark.

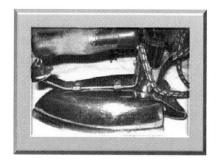

Tuesday was ironing day. The clothes that had been washed, dipped in starch, and dried on an outdoor clothesline had to be brought inside, sprinkled with water, folded up tightly in a sheet or pillow case to get slightly damp through and through so as to iron smoothly. The clothes were taken out a piece at a time to be ironed and hung up on clothes hangers or ironed and folded. This was at least one other long day of exhausting work. We did have electric irons (heavy irons) in my childhood.

The earlier non electric irons were very heavy and made of "iron" and were heated on a stove or at a fireplace. I never used one of those non electric irons, but my mother and older sisters did on the farm. I do not remember seeing my mother or sisters or anyone who helped us with the ironing use a non-electric iron. I have a small collection of flat irons on the hearth of my fireplace.

HOW TO WASH CLOTHES: Following is the "recipe for washing clothes" by an early American grandmother for a new bride. Despite the spelling, it has a bit of philosophy. This is an exact copy as written and found in an old scrap book.

"Build fire in backyard to heat kettle of rain water. Set tubs so smoke won't blow in eyes if wind is pert. Shave one hole cake of lie soap in boiling water. Sort things, make 3 piles. 1 pile white, 1 pile colored, 1 pile work britches and rags. To make starch, stir flour in cool water to smooth, then thin down with boiling water. Take white things, rub dirty spots on board, scrub hard, and boil, then Rub colored don't boil just wrench and starch. Take things out of kettle with broom stick handle, then wrench, and starch. Hang old rags on fence. Spread tea towels on grass. Pore wrench water in flower bed. Scrub porch with hot soapy water. Turn tubs upside down. Go put on clean dress, smooth hair with hair combs. Brew cup of tea, sit and rock a spell and count your blessings."

Ruth Baird Shaw

Christmas during the Great Depression

In the current financial crisis, people keep asking me about growing up during the Great Depression. Specifically, "How was Christmas celebrated differently?"

First, today we see Christmas decorations in stores before Labor Day. When I was a child, we did not start decorating for Christmas in September. Neither we nor our neighbors had the time or money to decorate for Christmas until Christmas week. Usually it was done on Christmas Eve. Our Christmas tree was a pine tree brought in from a nearby wooded area between our house and the Yellow River.

In my earliest memories of our Christmas trees, we decorated the tree with strings of popped corn, red and green roping from the store and homemade roping made of colored paper rings.

I remember as a child, lying in bed on Christmas Eve, trying to go to sleep so it would be Christmas when I woke up. Christmas was one day! Children in my day didn't have as much reason to be excited about Christmas presents as children do today. Or perhaps they had more reason.

When I woke up, there would be a stocking (one of my knee stockings left on a chair beside my bed) filled with candy and raisins (dried on the stems), a large red apple and an orange. There would also be some stick candy and chocolate drops and nuts, walnuts, pecans and large Brazil nuts. I might also receive a pair of warm gloves, a scarf or cap and a pair of roller skates.

We did not have bowls of fresh fruit and/or nuts on the table or in the fridge all the time as now. Of course, we had peaches, pears and country apples in season. But not large red "store bought" apples. Not oranges.

Oranges had to be shipped from Florida and were expensive and rare. My mother once told me how she and her little sisters would sit and eat their once-a-year orange and excitedly swap slices with one another. Bishop Arthur J. Moore, a prominent Methodist Bishop of my mother's generation, once told that "if one fell madly in love with a girl, he might share one piece of his Christmas orange with her".

My mother slicing one of her cakes to serve to family and guests.

At Christmas time, I remember Mama cooking a Japanese Fruit Cake. I do not have the recipe but the three cake layers were put together with two fruit and nut layers.

Mama's chocolate cake (still the best chocolate cake I have ever tasted) with her homemade fudge icing was my favorite.

She always made a coconut layer cake, an applesauce raisin cake, and several other kinds. Cooking and sharing cakes was one of the special Christmas traditions in our area. Apparently cake ingredients were plentiful and relatively inexpensive.

Mama always cooked a hen with dressing along with a ham for Christmas. Mama cooked only one turkey that I can remember. She bought the turkey alive. Chickens were also bought alive in those days. I remember that after Mama got the turkey prepared - its head chopped off, plucked, cleaned, dressed, and cooked - she had lost her appetite for turkey.

I hate to say it, as some of you may be on your way to a turkey dinner, but Mama never wanted to eat turkey again. I think the ordeal of preparing a smaller bird was not quite as traumatic as preparing a big turkey.

I have seen Mama wring the neck to kill a chicken, then pour boiling water over the limp bird and pluck the feathers off a few at a time. Smelly! Then she would singe the smaller feathers and hairs off with a burning piece of newspaper, scrub the skin, and finally take the insides out.

Mama would never have been so wasteful as to skin the chicken, as I soon learned to do in my early years as a housewife and family cook. This would delete the "singe the hairs off" step.

Also, being a city girl, I could never wring the chicken's neck but found it easier (and I thought more humane) to chop the neck off with an ax. Just thinking of this has helped to make me more and more vegetarian.

Class Relations in the 1920s and 30s

There were many class inequities and much class consciousness in the 1920s and 1930s. Many things that working class people (both black and white) had to endure were not right by today's standards.

Celestine Sibley, columnist at the *Atlanta Journal-Constitution*, liked to point out that people in the South were proud to be poor and "working class." This meant they were honest and at least not "carpet baggers."

My cousin, Aubrey Simms, and I talked briefly about this when he told me how his father did not want him to get a job in one of the cotton mills only a few miles from their farm, even with back and forth transportation and even after it became increasingly difficult to make a living on the farm and unions were making changes such as better wages and decreased working hours in textile mills.

The advent of World War II and the need for textiles for the army made it somewhat "patriotic."

No doubt the mill owners and officials were paternalistic toward mill workers. Mill hands! People were called "hands!" It is difficult to be intelligent (or so we thought) and perceptive and have to work 12 hours a day for barely enough income to survive. But in those early 1920 and 1930 days, people were thankful for any job, and no one seemed to have thought it was the government's responsibility. In many respects it was a continuation of the plantation system. But as I have described in other stories, textile mill employees were given opportunities that were not available to struggling farmers and people with other jobs or careers.

My mother (whether correct or not) felt that the mill officials tried to "run the church" as well as the mill and the town. So an employee looking with disdain toward the employer is nothing new.

I think Mama was right in that the Bibb Manufacturing Company officials probably did try to exert as much influence as possible on the churches. After all they had built three impressive "up to date" brick church buildings, a Methodist, a Baptist and a Presbyterian church.

It was the practice of the companies who moved their cotton factories south for cheaper labor after the Civil War to build the entire town including schools, churches, businesses, police and fire stations, community buildings and even swimming pools. They also hired a company nurse and brought in a doctor.

Probably mill owners and officials did the best they could for their times and understanding. When we look in the past to criticize or to re-write history we need to keep this in mind.

The mill owners and officials felt that they must look after their workers, some of whom were illiterate, unhealthy and superstitious. As uneducated and lacking in social graces as we were, I remember Mama being disconcerted at the superstitious talk and grammar of a few co-workers and early neighbors in our town.

Mama told me that when they first moved to Porterdale she felt that she had moved to the "jumping off place" in her strange surroundings. She seems to have thought of it as a wild and pagan town compared to life on the farm. The bringing of families together with other families in houses built close together was different from farm life.

Mama told me that she was especially interested one day to see that when the children would get into fights as they played together, some of the mothers would dash out of their houses, each taking her child's side of the argument. Sometimes the mothers would get into loud shouting matches and even physical fighting. Some of the women actually got so mad they "cussed."
Mama observed and commented on the fact that the children would often be back happily playing together while their mothers were still angry and hostile toward one another.

Mama had a good sense of humor. Sis (my oldest sister Louise) told me this story:

When we first moved to Porterdale, my young brothers, Charley, Tom, and Jack, were out playing with the neighborhood boys and got into a fight. One of the mothers came storming to our door, saying, "Miz Baird, I've come to 'whoop' you!"

Mama opened the door and calmly said, "Well, come right in, Mrs. Smith, and tell me what I've done to need a whipping."

Sis was happy to report that Mama made friends with the woman and did not get "whooped."

Speaking of cursing or "bad words" as we called it, I never heard even slang at home and rarely in the neighborhood. One day when the little boys were playing out in front of our house at 32 Hazel Street (the larger house we lived in before my father died), I heard my brother Jack say, "Oh, heck!" I was shocked. Jack was always ahead of the times. But his serious little sister was concerned for his immortal soul! I was seven or younger at the time, and Jack was about twelve.

My brother, Jack, taught me to skate and picked me up when I fell down. Our community had wonderful sidewalks that were perfect for walking to school, church or the one grocery store, the one drug store or the one dry goods store. They were also great for a street full of roller skaters.

Before I started to school, my parents had moved to a house on Hazel Street. Our neighbors on Hazel Street were hard-working church folks and, like my parents, although unschooled by today's standards, were intelligent with old-fashioned common sense and a strong Protestant work ethic.

They did not seem to consider themselves "victims," nor did they seem to be lacking in self-esteem.

For me, Porterdale was a good place in which to grow up. I became aware that some Covington residents, like my cousin, would have starved to death rather than take a job in a mill town.

Covington (our "town") was the Newton county seat. Porterdale was a village with three large textile factories owned and operated by Bibb Manufacturing Company. Covington also had a "Covington mill village" as a part of the town as did many of the cities in the South at that time.

In Porterdale, we also had two large red brick school buildings with grades one through nine and a "teachers' cottage" across the river but in walking distance to the school. I remember it as a two story house to board school teachers - a large, well-built and attractive house.

Bed and Bath in the Pre-World War II South

I never had a room of my own; not even a bed of my own. After Papa died, we moved to a smaller house. I slept in a double bed with my mother. There was also a single bed in this bedroom, and my sister, Mary, slept there. My brothers, Charlie, Tom, and Jack, slept in a room across the hall. My youngest brother, Jack, was five years older than I. My sister, Mary, was ten years older; so I was almost raised alone as far as sibling playmates were concerned.

This is me at age 4

Although we were poor, it was not "poverty" in the sense of poverty today. It is said that "poor" was proud (not un-Christian pride, of course) in the South after Sherman's successful march through Georgia and all the way to the sea. It left much of the South in ashes and ended the War Between the States.

My mother was pleased to tell about her grandmother who could (and did) trace her lineage back to the Revolution and her maternal grandfather who had been a prosperous land owner and a Methodist preacher.

And we, as well as nearly every Southern family, had a story of some brave woman or child facing the soldiers from the North, seemingly bent on burning the South to the ground and thus ending the horrible war. A few years ago, I read a part of our family history in which a woman ancestor faced Northern soldiers that were preparing to torch her house. She let the Yankee soldiers know that her husband was also a member of the Masonic lodge. Apparently this was a common ground respected by both North and South.

In our small town, most of the people worked for Bibb Manufacturing Company. Most were hard working and glad to have a job of any kind. All members of the family had to work to have enough income to survive. Families lived on their meager incomes and helped one another in times of emergency. Almost everyone we knew had about the same income and opportunities. If someone was out of work or sick, the neighbors collected money for them or made up a "pantry shower." There was no sick leave, and no one expected other such benefits.

My mother was hardworking and resourceful, and we always seemed to have plenty to eat and to share and most of what we needed. I do remember that on many occasions Mama was instrumental in collecting food supplies (pantry showers) for neighbors who were out of work because of sickness or other problems.

Mama also lent money (without interest) to neighbors between pay days. I remember that there was one man in the neighborhood who would make loans with interest to his less fortunate neighbors. This was considered un-neighborly and un-Christian.

The salary for a full week's work was $9.90 for some and $10.80 for other jobs. I remember people jokingly saying, "If you can't make $10.80, then $9.90 will do." We did "make do." To put this in focus, the overseers in the cotton factories were paid about $100 weekly. My husband's maternal grandfather, Charles Wilkerson was overseer of the "Card Room" in the Textile Plant in their small town and was paid one hundred dollars each week, I am told, so I am assuming that was the usual salary. The Card Room, as the name implies had machines with metal spikes used to disentangle the fibers of cotton before moving on to the Twister Room to be twisted into thread.

Each department in the Mill was referred to as Twister Room, Card Room, Spooler Room, Spinning Room, Weave Room and sometimes Weave Shop.

The overseers and other mill officials were given bigger and better houses to rent on larger lots in their own part of town. It is difficult for my grandchildren and the younger generation to understand, but the word "egalitarian" was yet to be added to our vocabulary. But we were looking forward!

In the bedroom where I slept with my mother and sister, we had a couple of rocking chairs and some straight chairs because this was also a sitting room. The parlor or "front room" was across the wide Hall in our house before my mother converted it into a bedroom to accommodate "boarders." This is another story.

Before going to bed, we sat around the heater at the "fireplace" and talked, or in my case, listened. If one decided to go to bed, one just went over in a corner or behind a door, undressed and put on night clothes. I remember warm flannel gowns.

Today we remind our children to go to the bathroom before going to bed. In those days a "slop jar" was brought into the bedroom, and the children were reminded to "go to the slop jar before you go to bed." Sometimes this vessel was called a "chamber pot" or just a "chamber." It was not my regular job, as I remember, but I often was told to "bring in the slop jar" or sometimes "go bring the chamber in." My mother usually did the more unpleasant job of taking it out, emptying it in the commode which was in a bathroom off the back porch, and washing it out.

The bathroom had a large footed bathtub and a commode. The "out house" in our community was before my time. However, this indoor plumbing had been added to one end of the back porch after the house was built. This smaller house on 45 Hazel Street was one of the older ones we moved into after my father's death.

Every room had a fireplace with a mantle above. The fireplace burned wood and coal in cold weather. Before going to bed in cold weather, we would back up to the fire to get our night gowns warm and then jump into bed under a mountain of quilts.

At one point a gas heater was put in the bathroom, but this was in my later childhood. I do remember that sometimes, in cold weather, we brought a large wash tub or a smaller "foot tub" into the warm kitchen or bedroom to take a bath. The bathroom was not as well sealed as the other rooms, so it was not suitable for bathing in very cold weather. We sometimes took sponge baths. This involved bringing a large wash pan of warm water with cloth, soap, and towel into some private corner of a room. Every part of the body was thoroughly washed and rinsed but not all at the same time. Mama believed "cleanliness was next to Godliness."

My earliest memory of bedding was of sheets that were made at home with seams down the middle. I think that textile looms that would weave cloth 54 or 60 inches wide were developed much later. I remember a few straw mattresses. These were homemade mattresses filled with straw to put on beds. I remember such a mattress on a small odd-sized bed in one of the rooms. Probably there were no mattresses that size on the market. The other mattresses were factory-made, cotton-filled mattresses.

We were fortunate to also have feather bed mattresses to put on top of all the cotton mattresses. Mama was very resourceful. Feather mattresses were made at home. One would buy pillow ticking cloth (pillows were made at home also), sew it the length and width of the bed and fill it with feathers. On a cold winter night it was good to sink down in a bed of feathers and under the weight of numerous homemade and home-quilted quilts. In the 1930s we called them "feather beds" and put them on top of the cotton mattresses. This added to the bed-making time every morning. One had to fluff up the feathers and smooth it out, often turning it over, and frequently taking it out in the sun to "air it out." When innerspring mattresses were added to the market, most people were glad to retire the feather bed to history.

Homemade quilts? We had large stacks of them, home-pieced and home-quilted by Mama and the women in the neighborhood. In cold weather one was weighted down under warm quilts. In summer, when company came, quilts were folded on the floor to make mattresses for the children and sometimes for adults to sleep on after all the beds were filled.

We children loved these temporary beds. To make the quilts, quilting frames were hung from the four corners of the ceiling of our bedroom and drawn up at night. I have slept many nights with an unfinished quilt suspended above me. Neighbors would come to visit and help with the quilting. Any unoccupied house in the village was often put into service for quilting bees. The quilting frames were hung from the ceiling; and six to eight women would take a chair and sit on all sides of the quilt, making fine stitches in a quilt pattern that one of them had drawn.

There was much talk and laughter as these women visited while working on a quilt. The younger children played at their feet, and the older children were in and out of the house. The advantage of the empty room was that the quilt would not have to be lifted up at night and walked around in the daytime. In the evenings Mama would cut and sew various patterns for future quilting. The children would play around and sometimes be allowed to make a few stitches and were complimented if they could manage small stitches. If the stitches were too long, the mother would remove the stitches, often after the child left the room. Everyone took pride in fingers nimble enough to make practically invisible stitches.

I was allowed to make a few stitches occasionally but was not often invited to quilt, so I assume my stitches were far from invisible.

Ruth Baird Shaw

Fishing in the Yellow River

All four of my grandparents died before my birth. However, my maternal grandmother (Elizabeth Mask Dick) lived into old age and died only a few years before my birth. My sister Vera (twelve years older than I) told me about Grandma Dick visiting on occasion and how much Grandma loved fishing. Grandma would tell my sisters, Vera and Mary, to be good and help Mama with the housework and kitchen chores and she would take them fishing after dinner.

Vera told how she and Mary would do as Grandma asked and would help get all the household chores done. To quote Vera, "As soon as we cleaned up after dinner, Grandma would turn to Mama and say, 'Eula, I believe I will take the girls down to the river. They want to go fishing so bad!'" Vera added, "Grandma sure liked to fish."

Mama sure liked to fish, also. Perhaps she learned the secret of catching fish from her mother. Mama usually came home with a long string of fish. We either cooked the fish she caught or gave them to others to cook.

Many afternoons, when the weather permitted, Mama would finish up the housework; and she and a neighbor, Mrs. Parnell, would head for the Yellow River with Mamie (Mrs. Parnell's daughter) and me in tow.

The Yellow River was a long river and a nice place to go, especially in the summertime. In fact, my husband Charles Shaw and his brothers were fishing and swimming in the same Yellow River. It was 16 miles from his town to mine when traveling by car.

When Mamie and I went fishing with our mothers, we often dug the worms for fishing bait. We learned to dig where the dish water had been thrown out in our back yard after all the dishes had been washed. We put the worms in a can, adding a little of the dirt around them. If we did not find enough worms in our yard, we took a hoe with us and dug big fat worms near the river bank. Yes, girls could and did dig worms in those days. Real wiggly worms! We needed a great many worms for fishing.

Mama and Mrs. Parnell took their fishing seriously. Mamie and I soon learned our mothers expected us to remain very quiet so as not to frighten the fish away. Mamie and I sometimes fished, but more often our responsibility was to dig worms and talk in a whisper.

Nevertheless, we had fun exploring the woods, picking wild flowers or sweet shrubs and digging up rocks and "May Pops" while our mothers fished. They used long cane poles which they slung over their shoulders like pictures we see of Tom Sawyer going fishing.

I never missed an opportunity to go on one of these fishing expeditions but there was a problem. Among the lush vegetation near the river bank was a great deal of poison oak and ivy. I had long since learned not to touch the "three leaf" poison plant. Have you heard these lines?

Leaves of three,
Let it be!
Leaves of five,
Let it thrive!

Although I wore long sleeved shirts and overalls and came home to bathe in Clorox water, I often broke out into a painful, itchy rash.

Ruth Baird Shaw

The Civil War Parade

I love a parade! The first parade I ever saw was a Civil War Parade! I may be one of a few persons living in 2011 to tell of a parade featuring Civil war soldiers (1861-1865). The Civil War Parade passed down the streets in our small town when I was a small child in the 1920s. It was a small parade as parades go.

But any parade in our small southern hometown was exciting. This 1920s parade featured the soldiers who had answered the call to arms and were the last of the "disappearing soldiers" who had survived the Civil War to come back home to a devastated Georgia and Southland.

In those 1920-1930 days, we still referred to the tragic Civil War of "brothers against brothers" as "The War between the States."

It is hard for this generation or even my generation of black and white people who finally won the battle for equal rights to put ourselves back in the time of worldwide slavery and class and racial separation. Today white and black people have associated with one another in school, church and work situations. Most thoughtful people have come to respect our common humanity and to appreciate our differences.

The Civil War Parade of my childhood moved slowly as it passed our house. There were a few horses and wagons in the parade but the three elderly Civil War veterans with long grey hair were sitting on chairs in the back of a slow moving truck. These Civil War soldiers were not waving or smiling but were looking rather serious. I was standing near the road holding my mother's hand.

I asked Mama, "Who are those poor old men?"

"Those elderly men," I was told, "are among the last of the Civil War soldiers."

These men had probably seen many of their brothers maimed and killed in an "uncivil" war of "brothers fighting brothers." General Sherman is quoted as saying, "War is hell." If they had not learned it earlier, who could deny the truth of his words after Sherman's march through Georgia?

Unfortunately, the American Civil War was seen by many in the south as a "states' rights" issue. We are told that less than ten percent of the people in America's southland were slave holders. Most of the slave owners were Caucasian, but records reveal there were a few African Americans as well as a few Native Americans who were slave owners.

History also reveals while all "Christians" were not Abolitionists, all Abolitionists were Christians. There is no record of any Muslim, Buddhist, Hindu, atheist or persons of other religions who had tried to do anything about the world-wide system of slavery.

It was through the Christian Bible that Christians finally became literate enough to learn that God is "no respecter of persons" and, much later, powerful enough to defeat the evil institution of slavery.

As G.K. Chesterson said, "the end of slavery was begun when Jesus died ... although it took the church years to become powerful enough to defeat the powerful slave trade."

Many of the Confederate soldiers had never owned nor even seen a slave. My grandfather, Col. William Baird, a Methodist "exhorter" and teacher, like 90 percent of people in the South, never owned slaves. Methodist ministers were prohibited from slave ownership.

The first battles for equal right were fought in Christian conferences. In fact, when Georgia Methodist Bishop Andrews' wife inherited a slave, it caused a riff in the church that separated the Northern part of the church from the Southern part.

The Northern members of the Methodist General Conference in 1840 took away Bishop Andrew's credentials without hearing about his plans of how to divest himself of slave ownership. The Southern delegates took the side of the Georgia bishop. The slave that Bishop Andrews' wife inherited was the now famous "Miss Kitty," and freeing her with a place for her to go was a problem. In fact, she continued to live with them after her freedom. After their death, she continued to live in her own cottage.

Rev. Bogan Mask, a Methodist preacher and my maternal great grandfather, is said to have bought one slave for the purpose of freeing him. This old family story is told in more detail by Ferrel Sams in his book of fiction, "Epiphany." In Sams' book he tells us the son of the former slave who was freed by Rev. Mask was one of the first African American medical doctors.

The Southern men had been called to arms in a war that was seen then by many as "states rights" and "northern hostility toward the South." In reading the tragic history of the conflict today, we know the issue of Slavery was primary to whether or not we could "live out our creed" and become the United States.

The few young soldiers who lived to return home saw their countryside devastated. Many of their schools, church buildings and homes had been destroyed.

At age 88, I am the youngest and the only living granddaughter of William Baird, a Confederate Army officer in the Civil War. My father, Benjamin Wilson Baird, was the youngest son of Col. William Baird and his wife, Mary Marks Baird. I am the youngest of the 11 children born to Wilson and Ieula Ann Dick Baird. My father, Benjamin Wilson Baird, was 63 when I was born.

William Baird was wounded in the Battle of the Wilderness in North Carolina. His daughter's husband had been killed in the war, leaving her with a child to raise. My dad stayed on the farm to help his wounded father, mother and widowed sister and did not marry until he was forty.

Most of my contemporaries are three generations removed from the Civil War. My husband had two great-grandfathers in the Confederate Army. However, although I am four years younger than my husband, I was only two generations removed from the tragic toll of that war.

I thought of that Civil War Parade of my early childhood with its few surviving elderly Civil War soldiers recently while reading about the rapid disappearance of our American World War II (1941-1945) generation. My generation! The World War II generation includes my husband, Charles Shaw, and my brothers, Jackson Irvin Baird and John Thomas Baird. They, along with many school friends, went off to World War II. Young men were drafted to fight in response to Hitler's attack on Europe beginning with France and then Japan's deadly attack on America at Pearl Harbor on December 7, 1941.

My husband and brothers lived to come home. Four of my school classmates were killed: Homer Cook, Carroll Adams, Quinton "Red" Cole and J. W. Rye. God bless their memory and the memory of all the young men (and the few women) that went off to fight a war they hoped would be the last war!

These World War II soldiers, part of the generation labeled a few years ago as the "Greatest Generation" are also now "the disappearing generation" as were those three old men in the Civil War Parade of my childhood.

Family History: Typhoid and Kudzu

Dr. Joseph Chambers was said to be a top graduate of Emory Medical School in 1899. He was said to have two professional claims to fame. One was his work with typhoid. The other was his part in bringing the Kudzu vine to Georgia. The picture above is the Joseph Chambers' house and hospital at Inman in Fayette County, Georgia in early 1900s. I grew up hearing about our accomplished Chambers and Mask relatives.

My mother's father, Charles Dick, died when she was a baby and while her mother was pregnant with her youngest brother. So she and her seven siblings were raised in a house on the Inman, Georgia farm of their maternal grandparents, Bogan and Mary Chambers Mask. More details are on my blog post about school in the 1890s. My mother always told us children that we came "from good stock."

This was at a time when the word "egalitarian" was yet to be spoken. I grew up learning in school about three classes of people: (1) The Upper Class, (2) The Middle Class and (3) The Lower Class. People socialized with their own class as well as their own race. When the segment about "Classes of People" was taught in our

Civics school class, one little boy said to the teacher, "We are middle class, aren't we?" The teacher did not answer. I remember realizing the teacher thought we were not middle class but part of the lower class. After all, our community of Porterdale, Georgia was a "mill town."

The Civil War had taken its toll. While most of the workers in our town and in the South had little to no opportunity for education or learning skills, the work of many, including what my intelligent widowed mother did as a weaver in the Cord Weave Shop was far from unskilled. The cord weave department, as the name implies, wove heavy material of various widths for military tents or to reinforce tank and airplane tires.

The accomplished Chambers family included the "good stock" ancestors of which Mama was pleased to tell me about. Even though the Mask family, the Dick family and the Bairds were "good stock" also. Or so we thought. As a matter of fact, most of our neighbors were hard working people of intelligence and high morals.

Unfortunately, Southern families had kept going downhill in educational and financial opportunities after the destruction of the South called "the War between The States." Mama's Chambers great grandparents had died before she was old enough to know them, but she grew up knowing and revering Uncle Daniel and Aunt Rebekah Chambers McLucus as well as Grandpa and Grandma (Bogan and Mary Chambers Mask). They were hard working farmers, managing large farms, and they were leaders in both the church and community. Bogan Mask was also a Methodist preacher who did not own slaves but was said to have bought one slave in order to gain his freedom.

One of the stories Mama told about her childhood was on Sunday afternoons when she and her siblings would watch for any young couple riding in a horse and buggy dressed like were on their way to get married. She said that on many Sunday afternoons she and her siblings and other children would run to Grandpa's house and take turns peeping in the window and excitedly watching as Bogan Mask performed weddings. Mama told me that her Grandma Mary Chambers Mask was a small, slim woman who always wore a neat little bonnet on her head and a long dress and long clean apron.

Dr. Joseph Chambers was said to be a top graduate of Emory Medical School in 1899. He was remembered by Sara Jane's Grandmother Overstreet as a very kind man with two professional claims to fame. One was his work with typhoid. He figured out that human waste needed to be buried at least 18 inches down in order not to spread typhoid which was a big deal at the time.

His other claim to fame might not be considered a good thing by Kudzu haters. It is said Dr. Chambers was among the first to have Kudzu imported from the Orient in the 1930s after farmers had lost about two feet of topsoil. Kudzu would (and does) grow fast and hold the dirt on the land. They felt it was necessary. Unfortunately, with no natural enemies in this area, kudzu got out of hand. But in the 1890s the topsoil did not wash away with kudzu to hold it. Dr. Chambers was a doctor by profession and a farmer by interest and necessity.

Music of the Spheres

My mother, Ieula Dick Baird, was born in 1885. She was married in 1903 and was widowed in 1932. Mama was only 18 when she married my father - a man in his 40s. I suppose psychologists would say she was looking for a "father figure" as her father had died when she was less than two years old. However, it proved to be a very happy marriage.

My father, a devout Christian and articulate churchman, became seriously ill with a heart-kidney ailment when I was eight, and died when I was nine. Papa had been bedridden for nearly a year before he died. Mama cared for him tenderly. She adored this man, and he treasured her. She lived until 88 and grieved his passing as long as she lived.

I have seen the love in her eyes as she stood looking at his large framed picture hanging on the wall over the mantle above the fireplace. I remember all the positive words she told me about him as I was growing up.

Mama told me she had cried inconsolably for many days after his death and had not been able to sleep. Then one night, Papa came back to her in a dream that seemed to her like a vision. She said he talked with her, telling her all about his welcome to heaven and the hymn that was being sung when he arrived in his Heavenly Home. She told me Papa sang the amazingly beautiful hymn to her, and she thought it was the most wonderful song she had ever heard.

My mother told me how she had joyfully sung the words over and over in her dream and felt sure it was a hymn she would never forget.

Mama told me that after singing the hymn to her, Papa put his hands on her shoulder, as he had done many times in life, and told her of his love and told her to dry her tears and go to sleep because he was alright and she would be also.

Mama said, for the first time since her husband's passing, she went soundly to sleep in peace, still feeling his hand on her shoulder and singing the words of the hymn over and over.

My intelligent and practical mother awoke refreshed the next morning and remembered the story above as I related here. But she told me she could not remember a word or a note of the hymn heaven was singing when her precious husband arrived there. She remembered only that it was the most beautiful hymn she had ever heard!

The Apostle Paul wrote: *No eye has seen, nor ear heard, neither has it entered into the human heart what God has prepared for those who love him.* (1 Corinthians 2:9).

Random Thoughts about Courtship in the 1930s

What do you think about the quote, "the poet looks at the world like a man looks at a woman"? One man responded to this quote in the "Word a Day" column by saying, "Does that mean poets are afraid of the world?"

One day, when the first of our five daughters was a teenager, my husband watched the smiles and excitement as she talked on the phone with a young male school friend. He remarked, "I wish I had known when I was a teen that girls were waiting at the phone for boys to call." When he was a kid, he told me, he thought he had to persuade girls to go out with him. He had no idea girls waited by the phone hoping boys would call.

In my childhood and youth, food was cooked from scratch and clothes were made at home with long hours of sewing with needle and thread or a foot operated Singer sewing machine. No fast foods. No washing machines – even in winter. Clothes were rubbed by cold chapped hands on a rub board and hung on an outdoor clothes line – sometimes freezing before they would dry.

Although those daily chores were more complicated, it seems relationships between male and female were not so difficult or complicated.

Life seemed good in our little corner of the world in spite of all the deprivation. The Christian gospel of Grace brought the beauty of much "graciousness" into our community. The Christian gospel preached by Methodist Circuit Riders and others, in spite of any flaws they may have had, brought about enough "civility" that we could build productive and civilized communities. We worked hard and played hard.

My husband, Charles, and I were teenagers in the thirties. I can testify that the thirties were not a time when boys were afraid of girls. If they were afraid, they were brave enough to call anyway.

The teenaged boy I married tells me that when he looked across his school gym and saw me, he said to his buddy nearby, "I am going to ask that girl for a date." A good line? He said he and his friends were taking a look at all the girls on my side of the large gymnasium. The basketball game was in his school's gym playing my school's team. We lived sixteen miles apart.

Are some couples just "meant for each other"? It so happened that Charles had relatives living in my town. I was a school friend of his cousin, Clara. Clara and I were not close friends but did visit back and forth occasionally. One day, a close friend and I happened to be visiting with Clara when Charles and his family came for a Sunday afternoon visit.

Charles was still a teenager and did not have a car but managed to get back to my town on occasion. It was a time when hitchhiking was common. Once when Charles was unable to hitch a ride, he walked the 16 miles.

His friend, Bill, finally owned a car (with a rumble seat) and the problem was solved. Charles brought Bill down to my town and introduced Bill to my best friend, Julia. Problem again! Bill and Julia got married two months later. So Charles was back to hitching a ride when he could

not borrow his dad's car. Was Julia and Bill's marriage so soon after meeting a bad mistake? Not in this case. They were happily married for over 50 years until Bill's death.

One late afternoon, Charles came down to a pound party. What is a pound party? During these depression years, the hostess would invite all the kids to her home for a party. Everyone pitched in with refreshments by bringing a pound of cookies or fruit or part of a cake or whatever they had on hand. The hostess made a large pitcher of something to drink – punch, Kool-Aid or iced tea. We played games that would be called "mixers" today. These games would get the boys and girls talking to one another. Parents were nearby but basically out of sight.

It so happened that it was at a pound party that Charles asked me to marry him. One of the games that early evening had couples to take a walk together. The walk was along a well-lighted street with modest frame houses close together and people all along the short walk. Not a great deal of privacy.

While we were walking, he suddenly turned to me and asked, "Will you marry me?" My reply was, "Oh, I am too young to even think about marriage." Charles said, "I do not mean marriage right now. Could we be engaged?"

In retrospect, I suppose it is laughable to think of our innocence and ignorance. But as young we were, we talked quite seriously about what we expected in marriage. As they say, "the rest is history."

School Days, School Days, Dear Old Golden Rule Days

School days in the late 1920s and early 1930s could well be described as "school days, school days, dear old Golden Rule days." The "Golden Rule" or some other part of the Bible was read every day in public school when I was a child.

When I was in what was then called "Grammar School," we went to chapel three times a week. We referred to the school auditorium as "the chapel." No wonder atheists and agnostics want to re-write the history of America.

In chapel we sang church hymns and patriotic songs. We stood to place our hands over our hearts and pledge allegiance to the Flag of the United States of America. We prayed the Lord's Prayer and memorized scripture readings and repeated them in unison.

The large auditorium floor slanted down toward the stage and had theater style individual seats that lifted up so we could pass by. The floor of the auditorium was oiled clean and smelled of polish. We walked in long lines to chapel with each class sitting together.

I was a painfully shy child, but in 1930 I stood on a stage for the first time to tell a Bible story. I do not know why the teacher chose me. In my mind's eye, I see myself as a six or seven year-old, walking up the steps to the stage on the left of the large school auditorium.

I remember beginning the story by saying in rote fashion, "Once there was a sick man. He was so sick he could not walk. He was so sick he could not sit up. He had four friends who took him to Jesus."

I do not know why I remember so clearly walking up the steps to the stage and the words of the beginning of the story. The memory of the rest of my recitation is foggy. It is a familiar Bible story found both in Luke 5:18-25 and Mark 2:1-12.

Mark and Luke tell us the paralyzed man had four friends who took him on the mat where he lay to the place where Jesus was teaching. When they could not get into the house because of huge crowds surrounding Jesus, these four friends carried the crippled man up on the roof of the house, pried off enough of the tiles to let their friend down through the ceiling. Bible scholars tell us there was no damage to the roof. They placed their paralyzed friend at the feet of Jesus.

The rest of the story tells us that Jesus told the sick man to "stand up, take up your bed and go home." The man got up, picked up his mat and walked away praising God.

Field Days and Ball Games in the 1930s

In the 1930s our school participated in "field days" with competition between classes and between schools. This included relay races, 100-yard dashes, high jumps, broad jumps, etc. My brothers, Charley, Tom, and Jack excelled in all the races.

Charlie was a top student and Tom was one of the fastest (probably the fastest) runner in our school. It seemed that Tom often ran in his regular pants with shirttail flying rather than putting on the shorts and sleeveless tee which was the usual attire for field day competition.

One year Tom won a race for the school in his regular school clothes. It won him a great deal of local fame and became a family story. I thought Tom chose to run in his regular clothes out of "modesty" because Tom was indeed a modest man of few words.

A few years before he died, I asked Tom why he ran the race that Field Day in his regular clothes. He told me that after school that day, he had to rush home to lift Papa out of bed and then hurry back to school because they expected him to run in the race. Apparently he appeared on the school grounds just in time to run the race.

Tom was stronger than Jack or Charlie, so it fell his lot (or he may have volunteered after Papa became disabled) to lift Papa out of bed and then back into bed. Tom told me he would go to school every morning and answer the roll call. Soon after, he would leave school and run the relatively short distance home to lift Papa out of bed and into a chair. Later he would run back to lift him up out of the chair and back into bed.

Jack was also a gifted athlete in both baseball and basketball. My nephew, Lavay McCullough, recently told me this story: In baseball Jack played both as a third baseman and as a catcher. The Porterdale community had two teams - an "A" team and a "B" team. My brothers, both Tom and Jack, played on the "A' team and managed the "B" team.

There was a popular Minor League team in Atlanta named "The Atlanta Crackers." Once both of the Cracker's catchers had hurt their thumbs and were unable to play. They inquired around about "who was the best catcher in the Mill League?" and someone said "Jack Baird." So my youngest brother, Jack, was called to play a game for the Crackers. Jack had slipped his shoes off in the car on the way to Atlanta to play catcher for the Crackers. The man who gave him a ride to Ponce de Leon Park drove off with Jack's shoes still in the back seat. As it turned out, Jack, still in his teens, had small feet and the Crackers didn't have any cleats in his size. I am told Jack offered to play barefoot but this was against the League's rules. So Jack missed his big chance of playing with the popular Atlanta Crackers team whose games were always widely broadcast on radio.

This story is sad to me illustrating how the loss of our father affected Jack at such a young age. My husband, Charles, was Jack's age, and I know if he had had an opportunity to play with the prestigious Atlanta Crackers, his father, Grady Shaw, would have done whatever it took to get him to the Atlanta baseball field with the shoes and any anything else he needed.

Jack was also an exceptionally good basketball player and I, as his little sister, was always on his cheering team. I have seen Jack shoot the ball into the basket from the center of our gymnasium court many times. In the 1930s, height was not the primary criteria for basketball stardom as it is today. Jack was very fast and coordinated in basketball as well as baseball.

My friends and I walked to the baseball park every afternoon during baseball season. Tom was the star pitcher, and Jack the star catcher and their timid little sister their biggest fan. They worked well together. I often heard people remark that Tom was the best baseball pitcher around and could make pro if he wanted to.

After work, Tom continued to play on the town baseball team into young adulthood. Baseball was such a popular sport between towns that companies would hire good players for jobs just to have them play on their baseball teams.

Goodyear Company in Rockmart (about 50 miles northwest of Porterdale) offered Tom a better job than he had with Bibb Manufacturing Company in Porterdale to get him to pitch baseball for their team. Tom moved to Rockmart and met Rowena, the love of his life.

The Boll Weevil and Peanut Butter

I have written in another family story about my mother blaming the tiny bug called the "boll weevil" for our family's giving up cotton farming.

Cotton was king in the South and most farmers made their living by raising cotton. When the boll weevil infested the cotton plants, it wiped out the cotton farmers' profits. Many farmers lost their whole year's wages.

My father got a job in a nearby textile mill in Newton County and moved our family into Porterdale, a "model mill town" in the fall of 1922. I was born the next year.

Giving up farming for life in a textile town was a difficult decision. However, Porterdale became "home sweet home" to my siblings and to me. It was a great place to grow up with dedicated school teachers, as well as many church and community activities. My brothers, Tom and Jack, who served in the armed forces during World War II, talked with such nostalgia about their hometown, all their buddies declared they were looking forward to one day visiting Porterdale.

But Mama, in a time of class and race divisions, was aware that "mill workers" were considered low class. She said she first thought of Porterdale as "the jumping off place," a place where she would never have lived had it not been for the pesky, destructive boll weevil.

Mama loved the farm, and she sure had a "green thumb" in growing flowers in our small plot of ground as well as pots of flowers growing on the front porch.

Aunt Cora, Mama's older sister, visited from Atlanta a week or so every year in her old age. After breakfast every morning she would say to Mama, "Let's go out and sit in the garden for a while." She and Mama would walk the few feet out the front door and sit on the porch swing or in one of the comfortable rocking chairs amid the fragrant pots of flowers Mama had blooming.

We are told the boll weevils first came to the United States from Mexico, eating through Texas all the way east into the cotton fields of Alabama and Georgia. I grew up hearing the boll weevil blamed for much of the continued poverty in the south following the Civil War between the States.

When the cotton factory owners moved south looking for cheap labor, they apparently found plenty of hungry people, both black and white, looking for work. Early on, even children were hired for some of the jobs, and later as soon as they were old enough. The cotton boll weevil took people out of cotton fields and into cotton mills.

So I was amazed to learn that someone actually built a monument to the boll weevil in Enterprise, Alabama in 1919. The 13 ½ foot tall Boll Weevil Monument consists of a statue of a lady in a flowing white gown, with arms stretched high above her head to display a big black boll weevil. It is surrounded by a lighted fountain. It seems that two enterprising businessmen (H.H. Sessions and C.W. Baston) in Enterprise, Alabama determined that peanuts would make a good crop to plant where cotton had been grown.

Dr. George Carver of Alabama's Tuskegee Institute also did research to find as many products as possible using peanuts. Carver did not invent peanut butter, but he did popularize the use of peanut butter and found hundreds of industrial uses for the peanut plant. It is hard to believe that when cotton was king, there was no peanut butter!

I like the story Gregg Lewis, my son-in-law, tells about George Washington Carver's conversation with God. In Carver's words:

> *I said to God, "Mr. Creator, I would like to know all about the creation of the world."*
>
> *And God answered, "Little man, your mind is too small to understand creation. Ask something more your size."*
>
> *Then I said, "Mr. Creator, I would like to know all about the little peanut."*

Big men like Dr. George Washington Carver are brilliant enough to understand human limitations.

Albert Einstein said, "The fairest thing we can experience is the mysterious. It is the fundamental emotion which stands at the cradle of true science. He who knows it not and can no longer wonder - no longer feel amazement - is as good as dead." Einstein's view is shared by other great scientists like Niels and Bohr, who concluded there is room in a rational universe for incomprehensible wonders.

When Cotton was King

My father was in failing health when he got a job in one of the textile mills in Newton County (Porterdale) and moved his family into that "model mill town" in the fall of 1922. I was born the next year.

The first house our family lived in after moving to Porterdale was on Laurel Street which was a street behind the Osprey Mill Plant. However, it had the advantage of being near a lush woods and the Yellow River, a long winding river full of fish.

Osprey Mill was a large brick building and one of the three textile plants in Porterdale owned by Bibb Manufacturing Company. One of the other mill buildings was called simply, "the Old Mill" and the other, "The Welonie Mill."

The Bibb Company also owned the houses in Porterdale and kept them in good repair. They were generally considered nicer than the houses in many other textile towns. It was paternalistic but after Sherman's march through the South and the Civil War, most of the people in the South (both Caucasian and African American) had few educational or economic opportunities.

It was on Laurel Street where I was born and where Leon (my three-year-old brother) died in a measles epidemic. Leon became sick with measles as did I. I was about seven weeks old and had a mild case. Leon's ended in pneumonia and death. We must have lived on Laurel Street several years. My brother Charlie (about 7 at the time) told me he remembered the family's grief at Leon's death and Mama being put to bed (she had a 7 week old baby) and her loud sobbing.

Another time, I remember being in the kitchen of that house when I heard a crash coming from the front of the house. I remember going into a front room (I was about 2 or 3) and seeing my doll (a doll with a china face and stuffed body) broken on the floor. I looked out the open door to see a little girl, one of my playmates, running across the road to her house. I do not remember the little girl's name. She may not have been a regular playmate. Apparently breaking the doll was traumatic for her. In my mind's eye, I see her running away wearing a light-colored dress and bloomers. Bloomers were much like some of the playsuits little children wear today - a roomy undergarment with elastic not only in the waist, but also at the legs, which came down nearly to the knees with a somewhat shorter dress over it.

 I do not remember any reaction of her or my family over the broken doll on the floor on Laurel Street. However, I remember the traumatic incident more than 80 years later. A doll was an expensive and treasured toy in those days when toys were few and far between. No doubt I was devastated to see this doll broken.

I also have a vague memory of walking in the woods behind Laurel Street holding my father's hand and picking wild flowers. Wild flowers were the only ones I would pick because my mother had instilled in me a deep respect for private property as well as a love for flowers.

My mother told me that in our late afternoon walks down the street when I was a tiny child, I would always stop, bend over, and smell all the flowers near the sidewalk, but I never picked one. We were taught not to pick flowers from gardens except our own.

I was to learn later that we do not have to own flowers to enjoy the sight and smell of them. In a real sense, as I later wrote in a poem about flowers we do not have to "own" beautiful flowers to enjoy the sight and smell of the world's treasures. In one sense "all that I see, belongs to me."

Canning in the Summertime

In my early childhood there were no electric refrigerators and, of course, no freezers or frozen food. In the summertime, ice wagons came daily to sell ice for the ice box to keep food cold. The only way to preserve surplus food was canning or drying. I remember the advent of our first electric refrigerator and the excitement of that first refrigerator. We had one neighbor who, when hearing the buzz of the electricity coming from the new refrigerator in our kitchen would say with awe, "It's making more ice."

During the summer the large iron stove would have to be fired up to make fig, pear and peach preserves and apple jelly. Mama would dry apples and peaches for winter pies and make applesauce, peach and pear preserves and pickles.

We had a beautiful little peach tree in our back yard near the street. Often when little boys passed, they could not resist the temptation to pick some of the peaches. My mother loved children, including little boys. She had five sons, two of which were grown and married in my early memories. So Mama would go out and kindly tell the little boys to help her watch for the peaches to get ripe and to please let the peaches stay on the trees until they were ripe and she would share with them.

Nevertheless, "boys will be boys" as they say. By the time the peaches were ripe, there were usually not many still on the tree. But Mama always found enough on the yard side of the little tree, to make a few quart jars of some of the best peach pickles I ever ate.

My mother would also make a year's supply of jelly by putting apples and other fruit and peach or pear peelings in a large pot to boil and strain the juice. She also canned green beans, tomatoes and vegetable soup in large quantities.

I have seen Mama stand at the stove canning and preserving summer fruits and vegetables with sweat pouring off her face. She would have a towel around her neck like a scarf to wipe her face as she stood at the hot stove.

Canning made the whole house hot. So we escaped to the porch or yard as often as possible, as did all the neighbors.

One of the advantages was that with no television and no air conditioning one got acquainted with neighbors. As long as Mama lived, she had neighbors dropping in to visit, even in the television and window fan era of the fifties, sixties, and early seventies.

Sew and Sew

Among my early memories of the late 1920s is my mother sitting at her old Singer sewing machine, peddling away! Sewing was a vital part of her daily chores. She made her clothes - dresses as well as cotton slips.

Mama also made most, if not all, of the dresses and slips my sister Mary and I wore. And early on she sewed dresses for my two older sisters as well as shirts for my five brothers.

But Mama did not consider herself an accomplished seamstress as was Aunt Cora. It was said that Aunt Cora (Mama's older sister) could go into a dress shop, look at a dress, then come home and make a duplicate.

Mama always said she did just "plain sewing." However, I remember the younger women in the neighborhood would often come to get Mama's help with their sewing.

Mama told me she learned to sew, like Penelope, by "sewing all day and picking out stitches all night." She said she just "kept dabbling with it until I got it right." She did get it right. Her finished dresses were well done.

I did not realize this until later in life, but my mother never thought of herself as a pretty woman because her eyes did not focus properly. She was embarrassed that her eyes were "crossed." So she always wore glasses. She wouldn't believe it but people considered her beautiful, and she had a good figure even into old age.

One of the stories I remember from childhood is about a neighbor lady who came over one day to borrow a pattern to make a dress like Mama had made for herself. After the lady left with the pattern, my father turned to Mama and said, "She need not think when she finishes her dress like yours, she will look as good in the dress as you do."

Perhaps this helps to explain why Mama never found any fault with Papa! I told this story in a sermon one Father's Day in East Point United Methodist Church to illustrate the fact that Christian men usually know how to love and treat a woman. A few compliments go a long way! Following the Golden Rule would solve many of our problems in interpersonal relationships. My sister, Vera, told me that Mama and Papa were in love all their lives.

Cotton print dresses were the usual daily attire for women in our small town. These outfits had to be washed, starched, and ironed. No drip-dries nor wrinkle-proof material in those days.

I especially remember Mama working against a deadline to get my Girl Reserve Camp dresses finished. Every year, we made a long train trip to Savannah. The first time I saw the ocean was on one such trip. The first time I ate in a restaurant was on a Girl Reserve trip to Savannah. This was an event that required preparation.

Mama was always working with some of the other mothers in the neighborhood to get us girls ready for camp. In my memory I see Mama sitting at the old sewing machine and peddling away with Blanche Fincher and other young mothers in the room consulting with one another about how the Girl Reserve dresses and scarves needed to be fashioned just right for the event. Each little girl was to pack two white dresses with blue scarfs and two blue dresses with white scarfs to wear for the trip.

Ann Southern and Me

At one point after the death of my father, my mother took in boarders. The sofa in the living room (called the "front room" or "parlor") was brought into the wide hall that went down the middle of the house and beds were set up in the front room to make a bedroom for the boarders.

The women boarders slept in this bedroom (our former parlor) across the hall from where my mother, my sister Mary and I slept.

I remember also a young man that came by looking for room and board. Mama put him in the bedroom with my brothers. This was a needed service in those days and a way for a widow to make extra money. Mama cooked regular meals and the boarders ate at the table with us.

My mother provided room and board for two to four people for several years and thus increased the family income. There was no Social Security or welfare, and borrowing would have been unthinkable. Mama was a talented and innovative woman who still had children to support.

One thing I remember about the boarders was being embarrassed almost to tears one day when they laughed at me.

When I was about twelve, someone had told me that I looked like Ann Southern, a current movie star. I had not seen her in the movies but had seen pictures of her in our daily newspaper.

WOW! I went home and stood in front of the large dresser mirror in the bedroom I shared with my mother and sister. For a time I combed my hair in several styles, smiling and turning back and forth at I primped in front of the mirror, trying to see if I really did look like this famous movie queen.

Suddenly I was brought back to reality by laughter coming from across the hall!

Laughter! I was one mortified little girl to realize that some boarders from across the hallway had been watching my antics in front of the mirror.

Women Recruited for Work during World War II

When my husband, Charles, was drafted into the Marine Air Corps during World War II, we lived in a small house in a small Georgia town near Charles' parents.

Every morning I dressed my two little girls, and we walked to the Post Office where I mailed the long letter I had written to my husband the night before. Then I picked up any mail I had as well as the mail for my parents-in-law. The Post Office was also the "Company Store" of Grand Ole Opry fame. So I bought any grocery items my mother-in-law or I needed. We had ration books and were limited in the amount of staples we could purchase.

On the way back home, I stopped at the home of my husband's parents for a brief visit and to give them any mail or information I had from their son or about the war.

They had another son, Grady, who was a tail bomber for the Air Force in the European theater. We were all "at war." Our hearts and prayers were with "our boys" in service and with the few women who were also serving as WACs or WAVEs. Women were not drafted, but many joined to serve in one of the Women's Corps.

Calloway Mills was making cloth for the growing needs of our defense troops in Europe as well as in the South Pacific, and soon cotton looms were running 24 hours a day to make tents and uniforms for the soldiers.

With so many men away in the Army, Navy, Marines or Coast Guard, Calloway Mills began to recruit more women workers. Then they noted that in order to make it possible for able-bodied women to work, child care was needed.

One day, a Calloway official came to me and asked if I would take a job supervising the night shift of the Children's Nursery they were establishing. They told me that when they were looking around to find someone, it had been noticed how well I cared for my two little children. They were told that I would likely be good for that responsibility.

Calloway Mills, under the direction of a "Nursery Expert" had taken one the large houses in the community, gutted it and rebuilt it with play and sleeping areas for children in the community.

I accepted the job and the small salary each month -- perhaps the only easy money I ever made. The Nursery stayed open only about a year. I suppose this kind of public child care was new to our generation. Most of the young women who needed child care while working for Calloway seemed to have a mother or an aunt to take over in their absence from home.

When The Weave Shop Ran 24 Hours a Day

My father died during the great depression in 1932. When the Japanese attached Pearl Harbor in 1941 and President Roosevelt declared war, my mother worked as a weaver in the Osprey Mill in Porterdale Georgia.

The Cord Weave Shop looms ran 24 hours a day during World War II to weave the heavy cloth used in making truck and tank tires in addition to the usual heavy cloth.

Mama, an intelligent and hard working woman, became quite expert as a weaver in the Cord Weave Shop. She seemed to be one of the few people who knew all about how to thread the warps and looms to begin a new supply of heavy cord material.

As I understand it, when a bolt of cloth was cut off the looms to be bundled up and shipped out, a new bolt of cloth could be begun in a relatively simple way. But to begin a different width of cloth required the loom to be threaded in a different way.

During World War II, with so many men away in Europe or the South Pacific, the word went out to recruit everyone who would work in the textile plants. I worked for a few months and was assigned to work in the Cord Weave Shop and saw how Mama was exceedingly knowledgeable about all the workings of the warps and weaving of the heavy cloth.

Mama was no longer young and had deep concern for her two youngest sons who were overseas in the Army. My brother Tom was in the Army Infantry in Europe, and Jack was in the Army Air Force serving in the South Pacific. Mama was working in the Textile plant Mondays through Friday. She handled the massive looms with energy and skill. The woven cord was used in the production of tires for trucks and tanks as well as for tents.

Long after Mama retired and was no longer on the payroll, on several occasions the Bibb Manufacturing Company officials sent a car to her home on Hazel Street to take Mama back into the Osprey Mill to thread the looms for a new batch of cloth. She was always happy to go back into the building to thread the looms and teach the skill to other weavers.

I do not remember that Mama was ever paid for this service. But to Ieula Dick Baird, the lady who collected food for families "out of work," the woman who helped deliver babies or visit the sick when the need arose, the lady who told me we came from "good stock," this deed was typical of her. So going back to her old job in the Cord Weave Shop to help someone learn the skill was just another neighborly thing to do.

A Glimpse of Romance during World War II

During World War II, I made a week-long train trip from Georgia to San Diego, California to be with my Marine husband before he was to be shipped out for action in the South Pacific.

Charles told me that "girls" were a major topic of conversation among these young marines in the barracks. This close knit unit of men passed around and pinned up pictures of girlfriends and wives for the admiration of their brothers.

"The greatest generation" is a label that was later to be conferred on them. At this point they were just "men in the making" and still preparing for overseas duty and combat.

My husband was happy to announce to his buddies that a real Georgia peach was on her way to California. It was a week long train trip with crowds of soldiers and their wives as weary travelers.

Alas, soon after my arrival, I was quarantined at the Naval Hospital with Scarlet Fever. My Marine could only come over to sit on a wall outside the hospital window and look longingly inside and speak through the window.

One afternoon he brought a buddy to see his "pin up girl." On this afternoon, the "Georgia Peach" was lying on her stomach with her feet toward the window.

The only thing my husband's buddy could think to say was, "She sure has beautiful feet."

Living on Hazel Street

My older cousin, Aubrey Simms, told me he remembered as a boy of six, the very night in 1922 when my father told his father about his decision to sell his farm and move to town. The Great Depression had already hit the South!

My father learned he could get a job in one of the Porterdale Mills and move his family to Porterdale, a mill town near Covington in Newton County, Georgia.

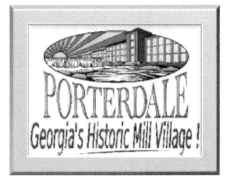

Aubrey told me about his father's continued refusal to move his family and have his children raised in a mill town when cotton farmers all over the South during the Great Depression and the Boll weevil epidemic were giving up on trying to make a living in farming.

Apparently my father, a hardworking and intelligent Christian man in failing health, thought this his only option. He worked in the Old Porterdale mill (pictured above) until he became disabled. The first house we lived in was on Laurel Street. Laurel Street was near the woods and the Yellow River.

My father was bedridden for over a year and died when I was nine. Among my first memories is walking with my Papa in the beautiful woods in back of our house and near the Yellow River, holding his hand and picking wild flowers.

I remember standing by his bedside in his final illness and two specific things he told me. He told me to always "mind you mother" and to stay in my own yard to play unless I had "leave from your mother." The second thing he told me was to always tell the truth because one's word was important. My father's Christian witness has had a profound influence on me.

Aubrey Simms and I both grew up proud of the same grandfather, Colonel William Baird, who was a confederate Army Officer.

My mother often reminded me I came from "good stock, " (at a time when people thought "class" and "race" were important) meaning our ancestors were educated and owners of their own housing.

I was interested a few years ago when Ferrell Sams, a well-known Georgia Writer and medical doctor from Fayette County, published his book, **Epiphany**. In the book he wrote about Bogan Mask as a preacher who bought a slave for the purpose of granting freedom to him. The grandson of the slave was said to be the first African American doctor in Georgia. Ferrell Sam's **Epiphany** is a book of fiction. But I understand this story is a part of our family lore.

We know "owning slaves" was not an accepted practice by Methodist preachers before the Civil War, even though it was a common worldwide custom.

It was in the Christian Bible that people of all ethnicities learned that God is not a "respecter of persons" but loves each individual - "the world." (John 3:16)

Before the Civil War (1861- 1865) many people who were wealthy enough and could not find enough workers to hire, brought slaves to maintain their property. In the Southern United States, less than ten percent of the Caucasians, a few Native Americans and a few African Americans "owned" slaves. The slaves were mostly people, bought (from other Africans) and brought from the continent of Africa.

Mama was well aware that the country and the world at that time, not only discriminated against people of different races but classes as well. The South paid a high price for its participation in what John Wesley and John Wilberforce and other literate Caucasian Christian men and women rightly called, "the unspeakable evil of slavery."

In our egalitarian society, we would do well to try to put these years in the context of widespread illiteracy and worldwide serfdom. People born into a world of class and race divisions accept it as a part of life.

I have written briefly about how my husband and I began to take some licks for our work for the breakdown of segregation between the races and approval of integration long before it became a politically correct posture.

As I told in another story, we were taught in our civics classes in school about the three economic classes: Upper Class, Middle Class and Lower Class. I remember one day when this unit came up. One little boy raised his hand and said to the teacher, "We are the Middle Class?" The teacher paused and tried to find words to get around the label.

Lower Class? But I was thinking, "Even in the Great Depression, there are people poorer than we!" There was a row of three or four "poor houses" out on Brown's Bridge Road near Covington where some old people lived in "poor houses." I understood they were old people, not able to work, who had no money and no relatives to look after them. One day we were riding out that road and saw an old man sitting on the porch staring at people who passed by. I was told it was a row of "poor houses." This house and the pitiful elderly man are both on the wall of my memory.

My brief memories of our life on Ivy Street include a painful bee sting and a new pair of shoes. I do not know how long we lived on Ivy Street but moving in those days with such a small amount of personal property was a snap!

We seem to have always had a porch swing which may have taken more than a few minutes to take down and move to a new porch.

I remember sitting on the swing on our Ivy Street porch when a bee sting sent me screaming to my mother in the house.

I also remember getting a new pair of black patent leather slippers while we lived on Ivy Street. I was walking down the street holding Mary's hand. I must have been about four and Mary fourteen. I could hardly walk for looking down at my new shoes. Apparently my delight with the new shoes embarrassed Mary or perhaps she was afraid I would fall down. Anyway, as we walked, she kept reminding me to stop looking down at my shoes.

We lived on Ivy Street until a larger house became vacant on Hazel Street which ran parallel to Ivy just one street over. We moved into one of the new houses. They were built to also be a duplex when needed but we rented to whole house. The back had three small rooms. The center room held a large footed bath tub. On each side was a smaller room with a commode.

Many of my memories of Porterdale center on Hazel Street. Mama lived on Hazel Street after Bibb manufacturing Company sold the houses and until she died in 1973.

We thought Hazel Street the perfect location. We called in "our corner." Wonderful neighbors: Albert and Blanche Fincher, whose children, Hazel, Dorothy and Lamar, were my playmates. Mr. and Mrs. Parnell were also our good friends and their son and daughter E.F Parnell and Mamie Miller. The Hornings with Guy, Sybil and Hazel. The Moores (Obie and Grace, Obie Jr. and Billie). The Martins, Capes and Loyds.

Mrs. Parnell had two older children from a former marriage: a son, Henry Miller and a daughter, Lois, who married Woodrow Rogers. Henry had married an older woman, a "grass widow." What is a grass widow? A divorced woman (of which there were few in those days) was said to be a "grass widow."

I remember Henry's first wife as very slim and with bright red hair. They had no children and later divorced.

As I remember, some of the women in the neighborhood accepted Henry's divorce from the "grass widow" without problem because he was, they reasoned, "not Biblically married in the first place." Today we consider this discrimination (a word we probably had never heard then), but I think the harshness toward Henry's first wife was that the neighbors felt this "older, more experienced woman" had taken advantage of the teenaged Henry.

Henry later married a pretty brunette his own age. I think her name was Maggie and they, in due time, had a son. I would occasionally go with my friend Mamie to visit them and play with the baby.

Other neighbors were the Hornings, who had a son, Guy, and two daughters, Hazel and Sybil. Mrs. Horning's mother "Grannie Brooks" lived with them. Grannie Brooks was known in the neighborhood as devoutly Christian. I remember her as a boxlike short woman in long starched print dresses with her long gray hair pulled back in a large bun.

One day Grannie Brooks got very sick, and they sent for Dr. Baxley and Mama. This is the same Dr. Baxley who was first to "put women to sleep" before he delivered their babies. When Mama returned from Granny Brooks' house, I heard her tell my older sister that Grannie Brooks' bowels were impacted, and Dr. Baxley had "picked it out of her." Dr. Baxley must have been a kind man. Grannie Brooks had said, "Dr. Baxley, pray for me." Dr. Baxley replied, "Grannie, you pray and I will pick." This is definitely more than you want to know! It is amazing what children hear and remember!

The Capes, Loyds, Browns, and Martins were also our long-time neighbors on "our corner" of Hazel Street. We referred to this section of town as "our corner." If we had owned the house, the block or the whole town, at least from a child's point of view, it could not have been more "ours" nor more "home."

Oh, the benefits of lack of ownership?

Hazel Street provided a slightly closer walk to school, church, post office and the few stores in town; one grocery store and one drug store. The Pharmacy had a soda fountain with ice cream cones going for five cents. However, in those days, nickels had to count. We did not often patronize the soda fountain. It was a special treat on occasion.

The Methodist church in Porterdale

One thing I remember buying at the grocery store was a package of six small cinnamon rolls for five cents. As delicious as my yeast coffee cakes are, they do not compare with the taste of those rare cinnamon rolls of my childhood memory.

One day Mama sent me to the store to get three cans of salmon.

Ruth Baird Shaw

I started walking back up the hill toward home with the three cans in a paper bag and sat down for a few minutes on the steps to the Methodist church.

The steps to the Methodist church came all the way down to the sidewalk that went down to the General Store. I sat on the bottom step and counted my change.

As I counted I realized the clerk had given me five cents too much change. A whole nickel too much! I would have to go back to the store to give the man his money. When I handed the store clerk the nickel and told him he gave me too much change he laughed and told me the cans were three for twenty five cents.

The Giles Girls

Most of us have friends and relatives we love but who do not fit the regular mold. My mother had cousins that she and her siblings called the "Giles girls," even after they became prim and proper old ladies. The three who became the "Giles girls" or the "Giles sisters" never married. In fact before "political correctness" came in vogue, they were labeled "old maids."

Mama loved and respected her cousins and had played with them as a child. So we kept in touch and visited as often as possible as long as they lived, even though we lived some distance apart.

The Giles sisters were perfect housekeepers. Spotless! Their country house was said to be so clean one could "eat off the floor." I am sure no one ever did!

Annie and Lula were in charge of the cooking and Pearl did much of the "outside work", maintaining a large lush garden and a yard full of frying sized chickens. They raised their own vegetables for year round use and canned vegetables and dried or canned fruits for winter use.

I remember sitting at their table one time as a child with bowls of fresh garden vegetables, platters of fried chicken and a huge bowl of fresh sliced country tomatoes, not to mention the plate of perfectly browned cornbread and "just out of the oven" buttermilk biscuits.

Their mother, Aunt Elmira, was a sister to Mama's mother, Elizabeth. Elmira and Elizabeth were the daughters of the prosperous (for the times) farmer and Methodist preacher, Bogan Mask. They could (and did) trace their family history back to the Revolution. Family history was an important indicator of "class" and was valued in the South with so many other things "gone with the wind" after the Civil War.

One of the Giles daughters had married, and their only brother had married; but Annie, Pearl, and Lula never married. When Mama and her sisters, Aunt Molly, Aunt Cora and Aunt Fannie visited together, they sometimes remarked about how "pitiful" it was that the Giles girls had never married.

I was a child but remember Aunt Cora pointing out that it was because their papa, Uncle Bill Giles, was so "peculiar." They said Uncle Bill Giles was "curious." This did not mean the dictionary definition for the word as eager to learn or inquisitive. Uncle Bill, they remarked, was "flat out cure-rus" which meant strange, in that he would never let his daughters date. It was said that he ran off every man who showed an interest in courting one of his daughters. It seems that the youngest daughter, Martha, had "run off and got married."

I remember the Giles sisters visiting in our home a few times. The family lore is full of stories of the Giles girls. One of the stories tells of a visit when we were all visiting together with them at bedtime in the "sitting room - bedroom."

In the Pre-World War II South, we always brought a "slop jar" into the bedroom on cold winter nights rather than use the unheated bathroom off a side porch. I do not remember all the circumstances, but my four-year-old nephew was asleep on one of the beds. Lula said to Mama, in her slow speech typical of the Hollywood stereotype of the Southern drawl, "Eula, do you think it would be alright for me to use the slop jar with that little boy in the room?"

One of the Giles girls' specialties was quilting. In one of the bedrooms in their country home near Fayetteville there was a stack of beautiful quilts that reached all the way to the ceiling. Not just an eight foot ceiling, but a country ceiling! And the platform that held the quilts was just a few inches off the floor. When I went with my family to visit as a child, I was always awestruck to see such a mountainous stack of quilts. And they were folded only once, and the corners matched perfectly.

Years later, whenever anyone mentioned the Giles sisters, someone would say, "I wonder whatever happened to all those quilts?" I do not know. With no children or grandchildren to wear out the quilts, folded for sleeping on the floor, they may be heirlooms in some home. Hopefully some of the nieces or nephews have them.

Life goes on. God bless the memory of these dear Giles sisters who were such a fascinating part of my childhood.

Ruth Baird Shaw

Mama as Midwife

My mother was energetic and thoughtful. After my Father's death, in addition to holding down a responsible job in the Osprey Mill, cooking, cleaning and looking after her family, she was always ready to assist neighbors during sickness or childbirth.

In the 1930s, babies were born at home in small town Georgia. Our neighbors would send for the doctor and often for Mama. One day our neighbor, Mrs. Lucy Johnson (not her real name) had her eighth baby with the help of Mama and a doctor. It was a boy.

Mrs. Johnson, thrilled with her fifth son and eighth child, said, "I'm going to name him after Dr. William Baxter and Mrs. Baird." The baby was named William Baird Johnson. One reason Mrs. Johnson was so delighted with the baby and the people who delivered him was the new birth technique.

Dr. Baxley was new in town, (1935) and Mama told us that he "put Mrs. Johnson to sleep" before he delivered the baby. Prior to Dr. Baxley's arrival in town, Mrs. Johnson and other women in our area had their babies the old fashioned way - work (long and hard labor.)

When Mrs. Johnson woke up and realized her baby had been born while she was asleep, she was incredulous. Mama said Lucy kept saying over and over (still giddy from anesthesia), "I don't plan on having any more young'uns(short for young ones), but if I do, I'm sure going to have Dr. Baxley here -- and you, too, Mrs. Baird."

The "White Experience" during Segregation

African-American friends tell us it is difficult for white people to understand the "black experience." This was the phrase my husband and I heard over and over from black friends in the fifties and sixties in church and civic groups and in our home when African-Americans were visiting with us. It is true.

This lack of understanding by any of us who have not walked in the shoes of another is the stuff of which hostility and even riots are made! Perhaps some will find it interesting to hear something of the "white experience." Of course none of us, whatever the color our skin, can speak for all.

I was born in 1923, when the South was still trying to recover from the destruction of the Civil War and the beginnings of the Great Depression.

In our town, many Caucasian workers worked from "sunup to sundown," twelve-hour days for a meager living in one of the textile mills or anywhere they could find employment. Cotton farmers all over the South during the Great Depression and the boll weevil invasion were giving up on making a living in farming.

Textile mills had been moved south for cheap black and white labor after the Civil War. They found plenty. Many southerners can point back to the hard working "Cotton Mill" experience as a part of their inheritance.

Most of the black men we saw were the collectors of garbage or worked as unskilled laborers in one of the cotton factories. Many black women worked as cooks and housekeepers and in child care for the poor white workers. Sad to say, we each had our own schools and churches.

Most of our schools had been destroyed and school tuition and books for high school and college were beyond the means of most of the people, black and white.

It was customary and considered proper to socialize with one's own race. Thus black workers came into the homes of white people through the back door to distinguish it as a service rather than a social call. Class distinctions were also important, but were not always so obvious, nor so rigid. As Margaret Mitchell had Rhett Butler to illustrate in *Gone with the Wind*, with white skin, one could possibly make money by hook or by crook and sooner or later get legal and/or "respectful" and move up the social ladder. Possible, but not likely.

The white experience was that many, if not most, white men and women were also poorly schooled and worked 12-hour days. In those days, it took both paychecks to survive. Most children stopped school and went to work as soon as they were old enough.

When I came on the scene, this was the custom. This I saw and pretty much accepted in my childhood as "just the way things are." We had no social contact with African-American people at all. We had never heard the terms "segregation, "integration "or "discrimination." All the black people we knew were servants who seemed accepting of their status.

As a child, I had noticed that Mama always treated kindly the "colored" women who sometimes worked in our kitchen. My intelligent and hard-working widowed mother worked as a weaver in the Cord Weave Shop of Osprey Mill in our small town. The "Cord Weave Shop" made heavy cloth used for tent making among other such uses.

In those days it was a common practice for the colored or Negro cook to eat at a "cook table" rather than with the family. A cook table was a table on the side of the wall where we mixed and rolled our bread, etc. The dining table was in the center of the room and sometimes nearer the stove and therefore warmer. Mama would always ask the black lady, much to her seeming dismay, to sit at the dining table with us in cold weather.

I suppose this seemed the same kind of paternalism that white workers dealt with from textile officials who gave out Christmas bags of candy, fruit and nuts to everyone in town - black and white - and who built schools and churches and tried to be good to all their "mill hands." The textile mills jobs also required feet, eyes and brain but the workers were referred to as "hands."

We referred to Black people as "Colored people" or "Negroes" – often with the Southern pronunciation "Negra." We were corrected in school (and home) and told to fully pronounce the last vowel, "Negro." We were taught that it would be insulting to say "black," as in "old black Joe." And it was considered ignorant then as it is now considered insulting and criminal to say the "N word."

Incidentally "color," as on a color chart is not a good way, in my judgment, to define any of us. I have never seen anyone with "black" skin. On a color chart, skin might be described as dark brown to light beige. Neither have I seen "white" skin. Caucasians might accurately be described as having light ivory to dark beige skin. But snow is "white," and it is neither compliment nor insult for Christians to be told they can be washed "whiter than snow." We are taking about "soul" washing not skin. Perhaps one day we will describe ourselves as either Caucasian or Negroid, instead of the inaccurate description of "Black" or "White" or the divisive "European American" and "African American."

Being from a Christian family, I never saw any African American person being physically mistreated. But in addition to some kindnesses, I also observed some indignities against them. Whether we are African American or Caucasian, many of us are sad to know that our intelligent and good parents and/or grandparents had little to no educational opportunities in the south until after World War II.

When I was a young teen, an attractive and bright young "Negro" girl came into our kitchen and said something to me (not to my mother) to let me know coming into our house by the back door was discrimination rather than just "custom." I had never before thought about this.

My husband, Charles, 4 years older than I, remembered one young Negro man having rocks thrown at him as he ran away from "stealing" some apples from an apple orchard. Charles was a young boy at the time and didn't know for sure, but his fear was that the young man might have been seriously injured. These kinds of crimes against African Americans are tragic.

This made a profound impression on Charles, although he did not know the people who owned the apple tree or any of the people throwing rocks at the young man as he ran away. He said he stood there as a little boy feeling afraid and ashamed and knowing in his heart the horror of the situation. Charles and I often talked about this. This kind of behavior was foreign to the Christian concept and the experience of Peter and Cornelius in the Bible that God is no respecter of persons.

Even earlier, the Jewish law of gleaning taught that even a sojourner and a stranger was to be cared for and allowed to pick grain or fruit to eat from others' fields as he passed by.

Yes, there have been worldwide slavery and class distinctions from the beginning of written history. It was still a fact in Bible times but never condoned in the Bible as some have claimed. After all, the major celebration in the Old Testament is the Passover of the Hebrew slaves out of Egypt slavery into freedom.

After World War II, when things began to get better, and Charles and I became committed Christians, we spoke out for Civil Rights long before it became a politically correct posture for whites to take. We took some licks for this stance from those who did not see the need for such "quick change."

When Dr. Martin Luther King, Jr., A gifted Christian minister, began to speak out with conviction, many Caucasians became informed and educated enough to join him in his fight to the death.

Then in the Methodist Church we had white men and women like "Mrs. M. E. Tilly" and others who held Methodist feet to the fire until most of us woke up and saw the evil of segregation.

In the 60s my husband, Charles Shaw, was pastor of Trinity Methodist Church in Rome, Georgia. Silas McComb had been the church caretaker for many years. His wife died, and Mr. McComb asked my husband to participate in her funeral at their church, the Metropolitan Church, an African- American Methodist Church.

Miss Lottie Duncan, our Trinity Methodist Church secretary, and I went to the funeral. The people in the church welcomed us warmly. I observed they read from the same Bible and sang from the same Methodist Hymnal as we did. Why were we not friends and co-workers?

Perhaps we can recover from some of the bitterness when we realize the issue of slavery is not altogether a black and white issue. Less than 10 percent of the people in the South had "owned" slaves. Most were white but a few wealthy black people and a few Native Americans also owned slaves.

History reveals there were white Abolitionists who gave their life for freedom and civil rights from the beginning of African people being sold by some black Africans to some white slavers.
From my own experience, I know of many white people who worked and prayed tirelessly for the end of segregation and for equal rights for all people.

Today we see some white and some black "racists." Hopefully, it is a minority and most of us want the best life possible for all people.

Get out and Vote: Women's Right to Vote

This is the story of voting 90 years ago! This is about our grandmothers and great-grandmothers who could not vote only 90 years ago. It was not until 1920 that women were granted the right to go to the polls and vote.

Some women were jailed for picketing the White House, carrying signs asking for the vote. Authorities chained the hands of Lucy Baines to the cell bars above her head and left her hanging for the night, bleeding and gasping for air. Dora Lewis was hurled into a dark cell, smashed her head against an iron bed and was knocked out cold. Her cellmate, Alice Cosu, thought Lewis was dead and is said to have suffered a heart attack.

Additional affidavits describe prison guards - wielding clubs and with their warden's blessing – going on a rampage against the 33 women wrongly convicted of "obstructing sidewalk traffic."

Thus unfolded the "Night of Terror" on Nov. 15, 1917, when the warden at the Occoquan Workhouse in Virginia ordered his guards to teach a lesson to the suffragists imprisoned there because they dared to picket Woodrow Wilson's White House for the right to vote.

Some women won't vote this year because . . . why, exactly? We have carpool duties? We have to get to work? Our vote doesn't matter? It's raining?

My mother, Ieula Dick Baird, never learned to drive a car. However, she made a point to vote in each election. We need to get out and vote. Very courageous women fought hard for us to have that privilege. Whether you vote Democratic, Republican or Independent - remember to vote. History is being made.

Watch Out for Falling Cows!

My children have asked me to tell the old story of when a cow jumped into the side of our car when their dad and I were teenagers on a date.

The Great Depression years were a time when many families did not own an automobile. This was especially true in the South which did not begin to recover from the devastation of the Civil War until after World War II.

Charles's Dad, Grady Shaw, was a talented and good man. When he was finally able to buy a car, he took special care of it. Mr. Shaw was a generous and loving Dad who would often loan the car to Charles and James, his teen aged sons. As a responsible Dad, he always added instructions concerning their behavior and a final admonition, "Son, take care of the car."

These boys were aware their hardworking and involved Dad would always check mileage before they left and when they returned and inspect the car (and them) carefully for any signs of carelessness or abuse.

Charles was the oldest of five boys. His brothers called him "Buddy." One afternoon, Charles and James borrowed their dad's automobile and invited my school friend, Julia, and me to take a ride with them.

We were riding on a beautiful country road near Covington, only a few miles from my home, when all at once, we noticed an older farm woman in a long house dress and apron running with her arms raised, chasing a cow that had gotten outside a fenced area. The cow ran down the hill, across a ditch and jumped into the side and then onto our car.

As with most accidents, it happened in a scary flash! Charles stopped the car, but the last we saw of the cow, it was running away from the car but with a part of the car door handle still attached to its side. The first words James said was, "Buddy, what are we going to tell Daddy?"

What did they tell their Daddy? They told him the truth. Not that they were beyond stretching the truth if it suited their purpose in those days. But they believed they might as well tell their dad the truth because he had a way of finding out the truth anyway. Besides, this was too great a story for the Shaw boys to keep secret.

However, this truth was stranger than fiction and Daddy Shaw didn't believe they were telling the whole truth. I had to assure Charles' parents it was a true story after I came into the family.

Love Thy Neighbor

My father died in 1932, so I was raised by a bright, loving and hardworking widow in those 1930 depression years. Neighbors were an important part of life in the twenties and thirties. My mother used the term "We were neighbor to..." instead of saying "We lived near ... the so-and-so's."

We did not lock our doors even at night when I was a child. Neighbors were in and out of our home all the time. Often they came to borrow a cup of sugar or flour or an egg to finish out a recipe for a cake. A neighbor might stop in to share vegetables or cookies. Sometimes the visits were just to sit and talk. Our front porch was usually the gathering place in the evenings after dinner. We had several rocking chairs on the porch as well as a swing that seated two or three.

While the adults were talking, the children played "hide and seek," "kick the can" or "catch the fireflies" out in the front yard or on the unpaved road in front of our house. I have fond memories as a child of being in and out of the homes of our neighbors that visited with us daily.

Then there was a quaint lady from out of town who, with her children, would visit us overnight and sometimes for two or three days several times a year.

I remember sitting on our front porch (along with various friends and neighbors) near sundown one afternoon. We looked down the street and saw this lady and her children coming toward our house. I said to Mama, "Here comes Mrs. Johnson."

Someone asked Mama why Mrs. Johnson and her children often came to our house. They lived miles away. The answer seemed simple enough to Mama. "We were neighbor to them on the farm," she said.

The lady was short and heavy with her dark hair pulled straight back in a bun. Her only daughter and older child was Mae. Mae was thin and very subdued. She was even more timid than I. Mae walked just a little behind her mother on the sidewalk as they made their way down our street. The three little brothers followed in a procession. I can visualize them now as they walked toward our house.

Mama welcomed them, gave them supper and made beds for them. Mrs. Johnson slept in my bed. Mama then put pallets of folded quilts and feather pillows on the floor for Mae and me. Mama also put a comfortable pallet of quilts on the floor for the three little boys.

I do not remember what, if anything, Mae and I talked about before we fell asleep side by side on the floor. The lady had a husband, but we never saw him. I overheard someone say her husband was "sorry' and "no account." Children were "seen and not heard" in those days; so, of course, I did not ask. But I learned by listening.

In the days before TV, the comings and goings of the Johnsons was a mystery somewhat like a soap opera to me. The lady would always get up early, and she would come to the place where Mae and I were sleeping on the floor and say, "Rise, Mae." I thought this was "funny." Incidentally, we sometimes referred to mentally ill people as someone who "acted funny" or had "gone crazy." I thought the Johnson family "acted funny," and we both laughed and cried for them.

Looking back, it may have been wife and/or child abuse that caused them to leave home so suddenly, walk four or five miles and show up at our house. As far as I know they came and went without explanation. If Mama knew, she kept her own counsel and always treated Mrs. Johnson and her children with respect, preparing food and bedding for them as respectfully as she did when her own sisters visited. After all, they had been "neighbor to us" on the farm.

College Women in 1904 and 2010

Wesleyan College in Macon, Georgia was the first college chartered to award degrees to women. It was a Methodist school chartered in 1836 as the Georgia Female College.

The present name of Wesleyan College was adopted in 1919. These pictures are of our Cousin Blance Burch Harp's 1904 Wesleyan College graduation and pictures of other Wesleyan College's 1904 students.

Blance Burch Harp in her graduation dress at her graduation from Wesleyan College in 1904

How does Blance Burch Harp's graduation from Wesleyan College in Macon, Georgia in 1904 compare with college women graduating this year?

My granddaughter, Lillian Matthews Shaw, graduated from Mercer University, Macon, Georgia on May 29, 2010.

I do not know the history of the change from women wearing evening dress for graduation to the beginning of the cap and gown attire.

Lillian's graduation took place in the same city, just a few miles across town and 108 years after the 1902 graduation of her cousin, Blanche Burch Harpe.

Life

Our family in the Watkins Memorial parsonage living room in Ellijay, Georgia: (from l – r) Terrell, Charles holding David, me, Carol, Debi and Beth. Joan and Janice were away at college.

Our First Student Pastorate

In 1950, my husband, Charles, our four children and I moved to Kentucky for Charles to enroll at Asbury College to begin preparation for Christian ministry. Asbury was a college offering New Testament Greek for the undergraduate ministerial student. Charles' study of New Testament Greek continued later while he was a student at Candler School of Theology at Emory in 1954-1958.

Charles had come home just a few years earlier after two years as a Marine in World War II. He had obtained a good paying job with Calloway Mills. We had bought a house in his home town. So moving was a difficult decision.

To make it more difficult, a longtime friend and neighbor of his parents stopped him one day and said, "Charles, you are crazy to take your religion so seriously as to give up a good job and go to preaching!"

But Charles had a strong sense of the Lord's call concerning this major step. Soon after coming home after World War II, he had talked about this with our pastor, Rev. W.D. Spence. Rev. Spence invited Charles to preach his first sermon at Mt. Tabor Methodist, a small church on the same circuit with Charles' home church.

Then Charles was offered the opportunity to serve as pastor at the North Covington Methodist Church for the summer before moving to Kentucky. Charles had a genuine love for God and people, and so he had a good summer as pastor there.

Charles also had a good singing voice, and he became locally "famous" singing Stuart Hamblin's new gospel song, "It Is No Secret What God Can Do."

It Is No Secret What God Can Do

The chimes of time ring out the news,
Another day is through.
Someone slipped and fell.
Was that someone you?
You may have longed for added strength,
Your courage to renew.
Do not be disheartened,
For I have news for you.

It is no secret what God can do.
What He's done for others,
He'll do for you.
With arms wide open,
He'll pardon you.
It is no secret what God can do.

There is no night, for in His light
You never walk alone.
Always feel at home,
Wherever you may roam.

There is no power can conquer you
While God is on your side.
Take Him at His promise,
Don't run away and hide.

It is no secret what God can do.
What He's done for others,
He'll do for you.
With arms wide open,
He'll pardon you.
It is no secret what God can do.

~Stuart Hamlin~

In this little small informal church, they would take up a small
offering for the pastor each week. This was in the days before a

printed bulletin. Nearly every Sunday, Charles had his sermon on his mind and did not think of the offering. As he would stand up and open his Bible, one of the men would remind him, "Brother Shaw, you forgot the offering."

One unforgettable happening, among many, at that first little church, was on the last Sunday we were there before we were to leave to move to Kentucky for Charles to start preparing for full time ministry. An elderly woman in the congregation, dressed simply in a plain cotton print dress, came up to me at the end of our last service. She handed me an envelope and told me it was a tithe of her butter and egg money. She said she believed the "Lord has certainly called Brother Shaw to preach" and she told me she wanted to help a little.

It was five dollars! It did help more than a little. Every five dollar bill I have seen since then, even now, I see as money that has been on the Altar of God as someone's tithe.

We took as our theme song;

> "Living by faith…In Jesus above…
> Trusting, confiding…in His great love."

During his second year in college, Charles was appointed as a pastor of three small churches in South Ohio, the Portsmouth Conference. One of the interesting observations about the connectional church system is that a novice pastor is often the one appointed to pastor three or more small churches. Later, after more experience, he is sent to only one church with an associate pastor to help.

In the Portsmouth, Ohio area, at 9:30 a.m. each Sunday, we attended and Charles conducted the service and preached at a beautiful little church in the countryside called Cedar Mills. Then we went on to an 11 o'clock service each Sunday at Dunkinsville and then to Jacksonville Methodist Church at 7:00 p.m. The study and serious praying involved in preparing to pastor and preach three times each Sunday was an expansive and growing experience for Charles as a preacher, as a pastor and as a person.

The Dunkinsville Church owned the parsonage down the street from the church. It was a nice little cottage of 5 rooms and a path. The short cement path led to a comfortable, small "outhouse." The parsonage kitchen had a cold water faucet at the sink where we had plenty of cold water when we finally learned how to prime the pump.

Each Friday afternoon after Charles' last class at the college, we loaded up the car and made the three hour adventuresome drive to Dunkinsville. This was the beginning of getting to know and love many of the "salt of the earth" Christian people who make up the small church families who gather in church buildings all over our nation each week.

After the morning worship service at the Dunkinsville Methodist Church each Sunday, one family from the congregation would invite the pastor and his family to go home with them for a bountiful Sunday afternoon dinner. These dear people treated their young pastor and his family with love and respect and we returned the compliment. This attitude of cooperative ministry went with us throughout our active ministry in working with many talented and dedicated lay people in churches large and small.

At 7:00 each Sunday evening, we were at the Jacksonville Church for Charles to lead their weekly Sunday service. One of the unforgettable things about the Jacksonville Methodist Church was a remarkable elderly man who was hard of hearing but was determined not to miss a word of the pastor's sermon. So when the pastor started the sermon, Brother Brown would move up on the platform and sit next to Charles with his hand holding his ear out as close to the preacher as possible.

Charles finally got used to it, but the first time Brother Brown jumped up and shouted "Amen!" his young inexperienced pastor nearly jumped out of his skin and forgot his sermon.

God bless the memory of dear old Brother Brown. Several years after leaving that student pastorate, Charles and I had an occasion to go back through that part of Ohio and took a sentimental detour to drive by the Cedar Mills, Dunkinsville and Jacksonville churches. As we neared the Jacksonville church and community, Charles said, "I wonder about old Brother Brown – he must be well over 90 now and is probably already in heaven." Charles had hardly gotten the words out of his mouth when we looked to the left and there was the elderly Mr. Brown mowing his lawn with a push mower.

Charles preaching at the Mackville church

The next September, Charles was appointed to another student pastorate in Kentucky near enough to the college for him to commute to classes. He began his junior year at Asbury, driving the 30 miles each school day from the lovely parsonage in Mackville, Kentucky to Wilmore. Charles preached at Mackville at 10:00 a.m. each Sunday and at Antioch, 5 miles away, at 11:00 each Sunday morning. He also preached every Sunday night alternating between the two churches, again meeting and working with wonderful church families.

But we never forgot that first small church family in North Covington, Georgia and the first three small churches in Southern Ohio who believed in the Lord and believed that Lord could call and use even student pastors.

Our Methodist Parsonage Adventure

The Methodist Parsonage system has been both praised and viewed negatively by pastors and their families as well as by Methodist lay women and men - especially those who have served on their church "Parsonage Committee."

Methodist circuit riders rode west with the settlers and helped to build and settle this country. I'm told that since then there has been at least one Methodist Church in every county in the United States. Methodist pastors have always been and some still are "itinerants," traveling from place to place establishing and serving churches. Church lay people started building houses so the pastor, spouse and children could live in their community, often for no longer than four years in the case of Methodist preachers.

The first parsonage my husband, children and I lived in was in Dunkinsville, Ohio while he was a student pastor serving three churches in the area. As I mentioned earlier, the Dunkinsville parsonage in 1952 had "five rooms and a path." We had cold water in the kitchen sink when we finally learned to prime the pump.

Neither Charles not I had ever lived in luxury but neither of us had lived anywhere before without inside plumbing. But the path to the "out house" was paved. We welcomed this new adventure and continued to enthusiastically tell the Good News of Christ at every opportunity.

This photo is of Joan holding a rabbit in the back yard of the Mackville- Antioch Parsonage.

Ruth Baird Shaw

We always remembered, with a smile, E. Stanley Jones' words about all material blessings as "too good for a ransomed sinner."

After a year, Charles was appointed to another pastorate to serve two churches - Mackville and Antioch, Kentucky. For two years, we lived in Mackville's nice Cape Cod style parsonage in beautiful blue grass Kentucky and worked with some of the finest and hardest working Christian people in the world.

Charles earned his degree from Asbury in Wilmore, Kentucky where each ministerial student was required to take New Testament Greek. His Asbury education proved more than adequate when we moved back to Georgia where Charles enrolled at Candler School of Theology Seminary at Emory University in Atlanta.

Terrell, Deborah (on rocking horse) and Carol in the living room of Griffin's Midway-Sunnyside Parsonage

The North Georgia Conference of the worldwide Methodist Church assigned Charles to pastor Midway, Sunnyside and Vaughn churches in Griffin, Georgia in 1954 while commuting back and forth to Candler four days a week.

The Griffin parsonage was an old house. In fact, while we lived in this parsonage, Griffin High School presented a play about the 1920s. They put out the word requesting a loan of 1920 furniture for the set. Much of our parsonage furniture was moved to the Griffin High stage! But it was a wonderful old house with a small building in the back yard called a "Preacher's Study." We lived there four years while Charles started and finished Seminary and worked with and loved those dear people like family. I still keep in touch with some of them. Charles was invited back to preach at both Midway church and at Sunnyside many times for Revival and Homecoming preaching.

Since Charles death in 1986, I have been invited to preach at nearly every church where my husband had been the pastor, including Sunnyside United Methodist Church Homecoming and have preached the sermon at two homecoming services at Midway.

After Charles was ordained Elder in 1958, we lived in the spacious (4 bedrooms 3 baths) and beautifully furnished Methodist parsonages in Ellijay, Rome, Fairburn and Skyland, Epworth, Park Street and Forest Park in Atlanta.

In the front yard of the Ellijay Parsonage

By the way, at our 1968 Methodist General Conference, (meeting every 4 years) we became the United Methodist Church after uniting with the Evangelical United Brethren. In 1968 our family was residing in what became the Fairburn United Methodist parsonage.

Years later, moving into a parsonage alone was one of the most difficult things I have had to do as a pastor. But the beautiful and comfortable old parsonage in Grantville, Georgia was truly home to me for the three good years while I was pastor there. The residence was across the street from the stately red brick church.

In the late 1970s, the Methodist Retirement Parsonages that were available to retired pastors were sold and by the turn of the century, our country's prosperity began to trickle down to preachers. Pastors began to invest in property for retirement as more and more churches decided to get out of the "parsonage business" and budget a housing allowance for the pastoral family to rent or purchase their own housing.

A bit of Methodist History: The Methodist Church traces its roots back to 1738 when it developed in England as a result of the revival of Christianity under the preaching and teachings of John and Charles Wesley. While studying at Oxford, John Wesley, his brother Charles, and several other students formed a group devoted to study, prayer and helping the underprivileged. They were first called "the Holy Club," then labeled "Methodist" by their fellow students because of the method they used to go about their Bible study, prayer, fasting and work among the poor.

Both John and Charles Wesley undertook evangelistic preaching with an emphasis on conversion and holiness. It is said sermons were three simple points.

> 1. Everyone can be "saved." No one is predestined to be lost.
> 2. Everyone can know they are "saved." (Assurance)
> 3. Believers can live holy lives (Not absolute perfection but perfect love for God and people).

Though both Wesley brothers were ordained ministers of the Church of England, they were barred from speaking in many of its pulpits because of their evangelistic methods outside the church and among the underprivileged. They began to preach in homes, farm houses, barns, open fields - wherever they found an audience. Huge crowds gathered to hear the good news they proclaimed.

Wesley did not set out to create a new church, but instead began small faith-restoration groups within the Church called the "United Societies." However, the Methodist revival spread and eventually became its own separate church when the first conference was held in 1744.

George Whitefield (1714-1770) was a minister in the Church of England and also one of the leaders of the Methodist movement. Whitfield is famous for his part in the Great Awakening movement in America. As a follower of John Calvin, Whitefield and Wesley had different understandings of some of the doctrines of the church. The doctrine of predestination is one example.

In 1776, America was in war for its independence from England. With England and America at war with one another, John Wesley finally realized he must ordain Frances Asbury and Thomas Coke to continue work in America apart from the Church of England, which separated the Methodist work from the Anglican Church.

Mary and Martha

In 1979, Charles and I visited the Holy Land. On Sunday morning we drove out to the Eastern slope of the Mount of Olives for a worship service.

We had a breathtaking view of Jerusalem across the Kidron Valley. Alvis Waite from the South Georgia Conference United Methodist Church read the scripture and Charles preached.

Afterward we made a pilgrimage to see Lazarus's tomb and the site of the home of Martha, Mary and Lazarus. Who could visit Bethany and not write something about Mary and Martha?

Mary and Martha

When I was a child
I loved the story best
Of Mary and Martha.
When Jesus was their guest

Martha prepared
The bread and the meat,
While Mary kept sitting
At Jesus feet.

Somehow in the reading,
The thought was inferred
That women, like children,
Should be seen and not heard!

And I thought, like a Martha,
Stayed in my place,

Tended my household,
Took care of my face.

One day reading further
With a strangely warm heart,
I heard Jesus say
Mary has chosen that good part.

How I long to be Mary
Disciple devout,
While I'm more often Martha
Cumbered about.

Much hurry and serving
I stay on the . . . run,
For a Martha's work
Is never all done.

One day reading closer
In lovely retreat,
I learned even Martha
Can sit at His feet!

~Ruth Baird Shaw, 1979~

How Old is Old?

Two of the teen aged girls at Open Door Home in our city needed to interview an older person for a school assignment a few years ago.

Open Door is a home for children whose parents cannot or will not care for them. I met the criteria for "older person" so the Director at Open Door, my daughter Beth, called and asked if I would mind stopping by so the girls could interview me.

I went by and Beth introduced me to the girls. One of the girls was a 14 year old named Sarah. Beth told me, in Sarah's hearing, how proud she was of Sarah for making good marks in school. I congratulated her and expressed interest. Sarah immediately got her report card to show me. We had a nice visit.

When we started the interview, the first question she asked was, "To what do you attribute living to such a long old age?" Later when Beth was showing me out, she said she hoped the girls did not hurt my feelings by making such an issue of my age.

Of course, Beth knew, as well as I, that it did not bother me. When I lived in the Atlanta area, I was not as ancient as I am now but I often spoke to senior citizen groups on subjects related to aging as my undergraduate degree included a certificate in Gerontology from Georgia State University.

One of the persons I love to quote when I speak to a civic or church group about "aging" is Madeleine L'Engle. L'Engle said, "One of the nice things about growing old is you do not lose any of the other ages you have been."

Imagine that! Like Sarah, I know what it was like to be 14 and think 30 is old. I know what it is like to be 30 and still feel like 14! I know what it is like to be 30 and think 50 is old. And I know what it is like to be 50 and feel like 14 and 30. Now I am learning what it's like to be 80 and to know that 80 is just another number to add to the others. I am still all the other ages I have been!

As Christians, we know that at the end of the counting, a new day will dawn and the counting will start over. We gather in church every Sunday to celebrate the Easter faith that what we call "time" does not have the last word over what God calls eternity. What we call death does not have the last word over what God calls life. We march not toward the setting sun but toward the light of the new morning.

Have you Read the Latest "Best Seller"?

Reading the "best seller" is attacking cultural illiteracy. **The Bible** is still the world's "best seller" book. From a literary standpoint alone, there is no way that students can function today as well-informed and educated people without Biblical knowledge.

For example, a public high school English teacher said to her class, "In the short story we just read, there's a reference to one of the characters 'washing his hands' of the situation. Does anyone know where that phrase comes from?" Many students stared blankly, but several sheepishly raised their hands.

"The Bible," said one student nervously. (As silly as it sounds, some people are afraid of uttering the word "Bible" for fear of offending).

"Exactly," said the teacher, who went on to explain how Pontius Pilate washed his hands to symbolize that he was not responsible for Jesus's death and the meaning of the allusion in the story.

As a **Chicago Tribune** editorial put it, "Trying to understand American literature and history without some knowledge of **The Bible** is like trying to make sense of the ocean despite a complete ignorance of fish." Western culture was built on **The Bible**. Our literature, music, history, and politics are permeated with Biblical themes and Biblical language.

Commenting in the **Los Angeles Times**, David Gelernter asked, "Can you understand American culture without knowing the Biblical context of 'covenant,' 'promised land,' 'shining city on a hill'?" The answer is a resounding, no. Cultural literature begins with Bible literacy. **The Bible** and its influence is a great resource for anyone looking for a comprehensive academic understanding of the roots of modern civilization.

We so often hear the phrase "separation of church and state" as a reason to stop reading **The Bible** in public school events, but **The** Bible has been a part of school events from our founding until the 1960s. "Separation of church and state" did not mean that we were not to continue the historic invocation and benediction prayers at public school or "state" events.

"Separation of church and state "simply meant the United States would not have a "State Church" as they had in England. The Episcopal Church was then and still is "The Church of England." Our forebears chose not to have one denomination to be "The Church of the United States."

Growing Old

I am an old woman! Even if I did not know my birth date, I would see my age in the faces of others. It is interesting to grow old.

My husband and I married as teenagers and wanted a large family. After our youngest, David, was in school, I enrolled in college classes as a spare time activity or hobby.

As a pastor's wife and mother of seven, spare time was not readily available. I started as a history major but I aged into the study of aging. I finally earned a Bachelor of Interdisciplinary Studies, and in addition, a Certificate in Gerontology after our children had earned college degrees and married.

One day, while I was a student at Georgia State University, I was writing a paper about "growing older" for one of my Gerontology classes. I sat at my desk looking at the last two words I had typed. Two words; not just one! "Older" may be a word we avoid, but "growing" in one that opens up all kinds of positive possibilities.

To some degree, at least, we can choose to grow old rather than just get old.

My internship in Gerontology was at the Christian City Complex which included a nursing home, assisted living housing, an Alzheimer's unit and retiree homes. I saw examples of both kinds of aging. Some grew as they aged. Others just got older in fear and bitterness.

It is true that often when we walk in nursing homes and see blank stares and some pitiful conditions, we think "old" is tragic and say in our hearts, "Oh Lord, I do not want to get that old." However, statistics tell us most of the elderly live in their own homes and take care of themselves. The percentage of the "frail & disabled" is small - much less than 10% the last time I checked.

Regardless of our present age, if we live long enough there is an old man or an old woman in our future:

The Old Woman in my Future

Someday . . .Somehow . . .Somewhere in time
She's waiting . . . I will see
The old woman . . .Time is making
Time is making . . .Out of me

Will she be a sad complainer
A fretful tenant of the earth?
Or a kind, productive person
Filled with happiness and mirth?

Please be patient . . . God is making
Molding slowly . . . Out of me
A shining portrait . . . He has promised.
Just you wait and see.

He is smoothing out the roughness
Polishing the dreary places
Filling life with joy and gladness
Pouring out his gifts and graces.

God remake me . . . In your image.
I want to like her . . . when I see
The old woman . . . time is making,
Time is making . . . out of me!

~Ruth Baird Shaw~

You Don't Have to Shovel Sunshine

I have been a widow for 24 years. A few years ago I was friends with a man who had retired and with his wife had moved from Michigan to Georgia. His wife had been dead a couple of years when I met him at a church conference. He told me they moved to Georgia because in Georgia he "did not have to shovel sunshine."

However, last January, in our sunny Southland, we did have to shovel snow! Below is a picture of the Myrtle Hill Cemetery, showing the grave of Ellen Axson Wilson covered with snow. The picture was taken by Terrell Shaw during his three hour walk through downtown Rome's rare five inches of snowfall on the early morning of January 10, 2011. Woodrow Wilson described "Miss Elly Lou" as having "what splendid laughing eyes" when they first met in Rome, Georgia.

Pictured is the snow covered grave of Ellen Axson Wilson, wife of President Woodrow Wilson, in Myrtle Hill Cemetery, Rome, Georgia.

At this point in my life, I am glad to not have to shovel snow or try to walk on ice or snow. However, so many of our best family memories when our children were young are tied up with the few snow storms here in the "land of sunshine and cotton."

My husband and I were always as excited as the children when we had a rare snow storm. He would gather up the children and some hastily makeshift sleds and hurry to Shorter Hill or some other special place. Even if there was only a little snow, we all pitched in to make a snow man.

My job was often to stay home, prepare a pot of nourishing soup, put out a clean sheet to catch fresh snow

Raiford Crews, grandson of my friend, Ann Long, enjoying a rare Georgia snow in 2010

for snow ice cream, dry out wet gloves, serve hot soup and keep the home fires burning.

Today, as someone too old to shovel snow, I am enjoying the snow covered landscape on this second "snowed in day" and looking for someone to shovel my driveway and remembering "you do not have to shovel sunshine!"

The Seven Wonders of the World

The number "seven" is a good and important number to me and was to my husband because we are blessed with seven "wonder" children. It is interesting how many people will ask a couple, with a laugh, as if no one had thought to ask before: "Are you Catholic or just careless that you had so many children?"

We sometimes just smiled with the people who asked such questions. At other times we replied that we had hoped for eight children but had stopped with seven because "seven" in the Bible means "perfection" and "completion."

Once a college girl asked a more respectful question: "Mrs. Shaw, "was it your decision, your husband's decision or a joint decision to have seven children?"

Pleiades (plee-uh-deez) is a word taken from a Greek myth referring to the seven daughters of Atlas, placed as stars in the sky to save them from the pursuit of Orion. It can also be used to refer to a group of (usually seven) brilliant persons or things. It is a word I love! It reminds me of my husband's poetic words about each of "our seven." He loved to say, "If I had searched the ramparts of heaven, I could not have found a more wonderful baby."

All kinds of myths are written about this seven star formation. "Seven" continues to be an important number.

I read the story of a group of students who were asked to list their current "seven wonders of the world. Though there was some disagreement, the following got the most votes:

1. Egypt's Great Pyramids
2. Taj Mahal
3. Grand Canyon
4. Panama Canal
5. Empire State Building
6. St. Peter's Basilica
7. China's Great Wall

While gathering the votes the teacher noted that one student hadn't turned in her paper and was still thoughtfully working. She asked the girl if she was having trouble with her list.

The girl replied, "Yes, a little. I couldn't quite make up my mind because there are so many." The teacher said, "Well, tell us what you have and maybe we can help."

The girl hesitated and then read from her paper:

I think the seven wonders of the world are:

1. *To Touch*
2. *To Taste*
3. *To See*
4. *To Hear*

She hesitated a little and then added:

5. *To Feel*
6. *To Laugh*
7. *To Love*

The most "wonder filled" things in life are often the things we take for granted.

Ruth Baird Shaw

What do You Want to be When You Grow Up?

One morning in 2007, I drove out to the Livingston Community to visit with a young family. James and Mary and their four-year-old daughter, Morgan (not their real names), were a part of the church where I was serving as pastor.

Livingston United Methodist Church, organized in 1833, is in a historic community that was at one time the county seat. It is about ten miles west of the city of Rome. Rome has been Floyd County's seat for over a century, with its "three colleges, seven hills and three rivers."

Most of the people long ago moved away from Livingston church. It is in a picturesque country setting and is the oldest church in Floyd County. Livingston membership was so small we had only a few families, and Morgan was one of only two children in the congregation.

I had made an appointment to visit the family because the elderly grandmother - Livingston's revered oldest member who had been a member and leader in the church since her youth - was sick. James was at work, but Mary was on spring break from the school where she taught. I had a really great visit with Mary, Morgan and Mary's grandmother, Sarah.

Morgan, a bright and beautiful child, already knew her alphabet. She sat at my feet enjoying my visit and writing her name and drawing pictures for me and for all of us during the visit.

Mary told me that someone had asked Morgan a few days earlier what she wanted to be when she grew up. This precious little girl said, "I want to be a preacher." Mary told me Morgan sometimes would line up her dolls and preach to them.

The same question was asked of me when I was five or six. At that time, I had never known a woman pastor. However, if I had, I would have never and could have never envisioned myself doing something that required speaking in public. I also could not have envisioned myself as a teacher. A teacher had to stand up and talk! A nurse? No! A nurse had to give shots! What else could I plan to be when I grew up? I knew women who were wives. I could be a wife. I loved our Methodist pastor.

"When I grow up, I want to be a preacher's wife," was my timid reply.

Small Town Life for a Widow in the 1970s

My mother, Ieula Dick Baird, was born in 1885. She married Benjamin Wilson Baird in 1903 and was widowed in 1932. In the 1970s she was living alone in small town called Porterdale and enjoying her life fully. Why not? Her nine children were married and had families of their own and they visited her often enough. She was always glad to see them and never complained with any delay.

It was a time when women were addressed as Mrs. or Miss. Although her income was small, she had enough money to pay her utility bills, enough to buy any groceries and medicine she needed. Mrs. Baird always had enough money to loan or to generously share with any friend or neighbor.

She had electricity, a telephone and indoor plumbing - luxuries that were not available to her in her early years. She had a television that she would always tune in to hear Billy Graham and other pastors when their preaching was televised. She kept up with the daily broadcasts of *The Guiding Light* soap opera and read *The Bible* and the daily newspaper religiously. Her interests included politics as well as church news.

The Atlanta Braves! Mama was their biggest fan. She had learned baseball rules and lingo. She surprised me one day by telling me about another team "shutting out the Braves." I checked with my husband and learned that this meant the Braves had not scored a single run in the game.

Although Mama had a hearing loss, she turned the television up loud and listened until the game was over, even when the game continued after midnight.

One time a close neighbor (her duplex neighbor) complained, "Mrs. Baird, I cannot sleep with your television on so loud."

Mama told her kindly, "Mrs. Mathis, I am sorry but I cannot hear it if the sound is turned lower, and I am going to watch the Braves the few days they are on television."

Mama then went on to kindly explain to Mrs. Mathis how she herself had worked at night for a time and how she could sleep soundly in spite of any noise during the day by training herself to shut out the daytime sounds. She explained to Mrs. Mathis how she could shut out the sounds of the Braves game and go to sleep being thankful and thinking, "That noise is only Mrs. Baird enjoying the Braves."

As the youngest daughter, I visited my mother probably more often than any of my siblings. But she would tell me not to neglect my own family or my own church to visit her - that she was fine. But I would visit, and while I was there, do any shopping she needed. However, I did not worry about her too much even though I knew she had health problems because she had a "come to the door grocery man" and a "come when called doctor" as long as she lived.

Mr. Barkley owned and operated a small grocery store located between Porterdale and Covington. I was visiting one day when he stopped in to see what groceries Mama needed. He came into her open and unlocked back door after he knocked, sat down on a chair near Mama, took out his small tablet and said, "Mrs. Baird, what do you need today?"

Mama replied, "Mr. Barkley, I'm about out of apples." Then she added, "I need a sack of flour and some orange juice and co-colas and a few eggs."

Later in the afternoon, Mr. Barkley returned with the groceries, lifted them out of his box, sat them on her kitchen table and gave Mama the bill. She counted out the cash and paid for her groceries.

Mama also had a long time doctor, almost as old as she. This was great as Mama did not drive. I was told that she had been quite adept at handling a horse and buggy, but she had no interest in buying a car or learning to drive. Dr. Sams made house calls and was always ready to come whenever Mama needed medical care.

As Mama was getting to the end of her life, I had told her to please call day or night when she needed me. She called one day and said, "Ruth, I need you." I went down immediately from Atlanta to her home in Porterdale (about 45 minutes) and took her to the hospital in Covington.

Mama lived only two more days. As my sister Louise and I stood at her bedside, Dr. Sams said, with tears in his eyes, "I am so sorry about your mother." Mama died on Dec 7, 1973. She would have been 89 on March 6. Dr. Sams, her doctor, died only 4 months later. Mr. Barkley, her grocer, had a fatal heart attack a few months later and his grocery store was closed.

Pioneer Clergywomen

Georgia Harkness, Ruth Rogers and Me

I went back to school after my children were grown. In one of my early history classes at Georgia State University, a professor showed a great deal of interest in a paper I had submitted and asked, "What do you plan to be?"

The question of "to be" was unexpected. I had "already been." I was an older "sometimes" student, pursuing a hobby of learning.

However, when the question of "to be" came up, for some strange reason I thought about Georgia Harkness and Ruth Rogers. I suppose they were the only woman theologians I knew about at that time. Far back in the recesses of my mind I must have been slowly preparing for Christian ministry.

As a lifelong Methodist I had read Harkness' articles and had even filed some of her work. Dr. Georgia Harkness (photo on left) was the theologian who kept holding the Methodist General Conference's feet to the fire until in 1956 they voted for full ministerial rights for all qualified women. Her many books and articles as a Professor of Theology provide a wealth of information about her long career as a theologian, author, and clergywoman.

Harkness believed and taught that the issue of women's rights is more than a matter of justice. It is also a theological issue. What does the church really believe about the Christian God?

The theological themes that Harkness expresses in her writings were also lived out in the experiences of Ruth Rogers and other

Christian women who spent much of their talents and energy in trying to find a place to serve in answer to a strong calling from God.

On the issue of ordination for women, Harkness believed that ordination with all rights and responsibilities belonged to women as well as men and offered three reasons. Her first reason was a Biblical one. In Jesus Christ all barriers that separate persons from one another have been destroyed. She quotes Paul's well-known passage in Galatians that "there is neither Jew nor Greek, bond or free, male or female, for all are one in Christ Jesus." (Galatians 3:28)

Harkness further noted that ordination for women could be argued from a "practical" standpoint. She pointed out that a portion of the church's constituency was alienated and the gifts and graces of women were being lost to the mission of the church to the world.

Harkness remained aloof, as do I, to issues regarding inclusive language. The personal nature of God demands a personal pronoun reference. As Harkness said, "I see little sense in trying to change the terminology of the ages."

At the heart of her theology is a "responsible concern for persons everywhere and in every condition." This includes men! Her idea of

the partnership of the sexes emerges whereby the goal of shaping society in the direction of the kingdom of God relies upon mutuality and good will between Christian men and women.

In that same historical year of 1956, Dr. Ruth Rogers was the first woman to be ordained elder in the North Georgia Conference of the Methodist Church and my husband, a rising senior at Chandler School of Theology was ordained deacon.

Although my husband and I had sat in large Methodist conferences with her, I had never met Ruth Rogers until I, as Atlanta-College Park District Communication Chairperson in 1988, interviewed her for an article in the Wesleyan Christian Advocate.

The Rev. Dr. Ruth Rogers (photo on previous page, taken in 1958) believed, as do I, that the call from God is what makes a preacher, not whether one is a man or a woman. The deaths of two close family members had a great impact on her. Ruth Rogers had adopted a nephew, but in 1945 lost him at the age of 14 to bone cancer. Among his last words to her, "Aunt Ruth, you are going to have to do my preaching." Then in 1947, her beloved mother died in her arms saying, "Don't you see Christ? I can see him. He's right on the edge of a crowd. He's opening the eyes of the blind."

After the death of her son, Billy, Dr. Rogers did a great deal of thinking "and more praying" about it, but was not quite willing "to take on the enmity..." - to answer the call to preach. But after the experience of Christ at her mother's death bed, Rogers, who came from a family of Methodist ministers, said: "I felt I had to tell the story whether I wanted to or not." After she preached at a District Conference, the vote was unanimous to accept her call. But she was to learn that the enmity against women as preachers did not stop there.

When I interviewed her, Rogers was 84 years old and walked on crutches because of a fall on ice at the front of a church some years

before. But she still had a twinkle in her eyes and a lovely smile and she indicated to me that she has forgiven those who rejected her for whatever reason.

And I? (photo on left, taken in 2004) I was a happy wife, a devoted mother and an enthusiastic teacher of women's mission studies and Sunday School Bible lessons! I was unaware that Georgia Harkness and Ruth Rogers were paving roads over which I would one day be called to travel.

How can I briefly tell the story that led to my identity as pastor and as theology student? The path that led to that incredible day in December 1986 when I first stood in the pulpit of a United Methodist Church as "pastor" and to a bewildering day in Chandler's Commons in August 1987 as "student."

Go with me briefly to my childhood. I am nine years old and my father is dying. He has been ill for a year with a heart and kidney ailment. He is a committed Christian. Earlier, he had put his arm around me as I stood by his bedside and told me to never leave our yard without "leave" from my mother. Then he reminded me to always tell the truth and went on to explain the importance of truth. I am profoundly impressed by the faith my wise and good father lived. I am thinking, "When I grow up, I want to be that kind of Christian."

I found it interesting to note that both Georgia Harkness and Ruth Rogers were also profoundly affected by a dying parent's last words and/or actions. Harkness had told in her autobiography about returning home to nurse her father in his final illness. He had asked about her many successful books and remarked, ". . . but I wish you would write more about Jesus Christ." Harkness understood these remarks to be a "directive from an eternal realm" and saw this experience as a turn in her thinking and writing to a more "Christ-centered approach to religious truth." (Gilbert, p. 18)

Two years after my father's death, I was sitting with my mother in a worship service at our small town Methodist church, the same church in which I had been baptized as a small baby. The congregation was singing an old gospel song entitled "At the Cross." The song later fell into disrepute because of an offensive verse that went like this: "Would He (Christ) devote his sacred head for such a worm as I?" The hymnal committee later deleted "such a worm as I" and substituted "sinner such as I." I do not know about changing the words of a poem after the author's death but I, along with the hymnal committee did not know any "worm like" people. We didn't even lock our doors at night in my home town. The Psalmist had written that we were created just a little lower than angels!

But one phrase did capture my attention during the singing and I began to ponder the first theological question I ever remember giving thought to. It is a big one. As the singing continued, I was listening to: "Was it for crimes that I have done, Christ died upon the tree?" I thought, "How could my sins today have anything to do with the death of Jesus on the cross nearly 2000 years ago?" Yes! The mystery of God in Jesus Christ became a real part of my life - my story."

This was before Hitler, the Holocaust and World War II. The New Deal was beginning to work. Education was going to do away with crime, disease, and discrimination. Later, when I read about the extent of Hitler's crimes I thought back to that day in church. "Is it possible," I thought with great sadness, "For human beings to act like 'worms?'" The jury is in. Education and prosperity are not enough. Germany and Japan excelled in both education and prosperity when they plunged us into World War II. Only Christ can solve our sin problem.

Becoming a preacher is the last thing I ever expected or aspired to do. Charles recognized my call to preach early on and mentioned it to me in 1975 - before I said anything to him about it. He, as pastor, and the church (Park Street UMC) recommended me for license to preach, which was then and still is the starting point for ordained ministers in our United Methodist Church.

Charles began to have health problems and after a second heart attack and bypass surgery, he retired on disability in 1983. A year later the District Superintendent needed someone to fill in at Rico Church in Palmetto and called one Sunday morning and asked Charles to go down that morning to preach and conduct the service. He did and kept preaching every Sunday except on two occasions when he asked me to go down and preach.

Charles preached his last sermon the first Sunday in advent in 1986 and 3 days later "went home to be with the Lord." Two weeks later the District Superintendent called me and told me the congregation had asked to have me appointed to finish the conference year. The Bishop and Cabinet agreed. Would I do it? After much prayer, I knew this was an open door the Lord wanted me to walk through.

In spite of grief and responsibilities, I began as their pastor the 4th Sunday in Advent and continued to serve as pastor at Rico while I started and finished the work for a Master of Divinity degree from Candler School of Theology at Emory.

During my years of "telling the good news of Jesus" behind a pulpit instead of a Sunday school classroom or a Missionary platform, I have sought to learn how to communicate this good news of Jesus. The love and power of God in the hearts of people is able to bring people together across all kinds of barriers as Paul tells the people of Galatia in Galatians 3:22-28. "There is neither Jew nor Greek, there is neither slave nor free, there is neither male nor female; for you are all one in Christ Jesus."(Galatians 3:28)

Ordination is not a right to which any of us, male or female, are entitled. It is an unmerited call and an unexpected gift of the Lord's mercy. It is not a call to authority but a call to service.

BIBLIOGRAPHY

Gilbert, Paula Elizabeth. ***Choice of the Greater Good: The Christian Witness of Georgia Harkness.***

Harkness, Georgia. ***Grace Abounding***, Abingdon Press, Nashville, 1969.

Harkness, Georgia. ***The Ministry of Reconciliation***. Abingdon Press, New York, 1971.

Johnson, Helen. "Georgia Harkness: She Made Theology Understandable." ***United Methodist Today***, October 1974.

Harkness, Georgia. "Women and the Church," ***The Christian Century***. June 1937.

Life with Wings

Cecil B. DeMille wrote that he was in a canoe in Maine one summer day - just drifting through the water in a shallow place near the shore. He could see the bottom of the lake and noticed it was covered with water beetles.

One of the water beetles crawled up on a canoe, fastened its feet in the gunnels and died.

Three hours later, still floating in the warm sun, DeMille described how he witnessed a miracle. The shell of the water beetle cracked open and a tiny head emerged. The wings unfolded and finally a beautiful dragonfly with iridescent body and gossamer wings left the dead carcass and sailed across the surface of the water, shimmering in the afternoon sun - going further in a half second than the water beetle could crawl all day long.

The dragonfly sailed across the surface of the lake, but the water beetles below - unaware of the miracle of metamorphosis - could not see it. DeMille said, "Do you think God would do that for a water beetle and not do it for you and me?"

Have you ever known the feeling of being lifted above ordinary limitations? Not just doing the best you can "under the circumstances," but allowing God to get you out from under the circumstances that would hold you? God is able! God is able to lift us up and over the limitations placed on us or the limitations we place on ourselves.

One Sunday, I sat with the rest of the congregation listening to Charles Shaw (a great preacher) give a sermon. He told about an imaginary conversation someone had with an ordinary looking worm crawling down the road of a busy city. The worm was "out of place" but told the man, "Don't stop me. I'm going to get my wings."

I wrote this poem:

Ruth Baird Shaw

Life with Wings

God made the butterfly
And I…
Stand on earth
And watch it fly
And see that God
Has fashioned wings
For even earthbound
Creeping things!
I know that God
Intended wings
For you and me
Oh! My heart sings!
I've found my wings.
And even I…
Can over circumstances
Fly!

~Ruth Baird Shaw, 1973~

The Olympic Flame

In July of 1996, the Olympics were held in Georgia. On July 17, the Olympic Flame came to our town and created wild excitement and huge crowds as it passed right in front of the East Point Courthouse!

The historic East Point Avenue United Methodist Church is directly across the street from the Court House near downtown East Point just a few miles Southwest of Atlanta.

I joined with dozens on the porch of the church and hundreds of other people on the nearby streets to wave and cheer as the runner and Olympic Flame passed by.

It created amazing excitement! The Greek Olympic Flame means Citius, Altheus, Fortus! In English it means Faster, Higher, Stronger. The Olympic flame is an excellent symbol of the ability and discipline of human beings to excel by going faster, higher and stronger.

The Sunday morning after the Olympic Flame had passed in front of our East Point Avenue United Methodist Church on its way  down Washington Avenue to the excitement of cheering crowds of men, women and children, I sat behind the pulpit of our East Point Avenue church as the acolyte brought the Christian flame down the church center aisle to light the altar candles.

As I watched the acolyte bringing the Christian Flame down the church aisle toward the altar, I thought of the Olympic Flame with the great meaning of faster, higher, stronger.

And I thought of the Christian Flame and all its meaning of love, joy and peace which is still burning with a flame lighted over two thousand years ago.

How exciting to gather each week to celebrate the grace of God that has brought about graciousness and civility enough to build our great civilization!

The lighted altar candle represents and celebrates the amazing grace of Jesus, who overcame death and lives as the Light of the World!

Jesus is the blazing beacon lighting the darkness of our world with love, joy and peace.

Spring Magic

One of the Beatitudes, "Blessed are the meek, for they shall inherit the earth," seems to have a broader meaning than merely that mild people, meek as lambs, would ultimately inherit the earth.

Meekness is not weakness but a gentle spirit. In Greek, the word denotes self-control and genuine humility.

Our family lived in the Epworth parsonage on Claire Drive in Atlanta from 1970 -1974. It is located in a neighborhood so beautiful in the springtime that a few years ago, in a spread about the Druid Hills area of Atlanta, National Geographic featured an aerial view of the area with the dogwoods in bloom.

I learned then, as now, that even when I do not find the time or the garden space to make a flower garden, others do. So all of us are invited to share in the miracles and magic of Spring!

Spring Magic

I took a walk one April day
The Earth had turned to Spring
When I saw the countryside
My heart began to sing!

When I remembered Jesus said:
"Blessed are the meek,
They shall inherit all the earth."
Oh, let me join the meek?

My first draft; daffodils profuse
Golden gems - they shine
And make of simple landscapes
A treasured flower mine.

Lavender blankets of "Thrift,"
With wild extravagancy
Transformed barren slopes into
A Springtime canopy.

Tulips, pansies, hyacinths,
With rare perfume they bring
Glorious resurgence and
Priceless smells of Spring.

The Dogwood trees keep writing
Blank checks from the sod.
I draw up close enough to see
The signature of God!

Oh, I don't need a written deed
To claim my legacy
The flowering earth I hold in trust
All that I see...belongs to me!

~Ruth Baird Shaw, 1972~

Winter is an etching, spring a watercolor, summer an oil painting and autumn a mosaic of them all.

~Stanley Horowitz~

Wit's End Corner

My mother was still in her forties when my father died after being bedridden for a year. My father was a man of strong faith and knew the heartache and possible hardships his wife and children would have to endure after his death.

A few days before Papa died, he gave my mother a poem entitled "Wit's End Corner" that he had cut out of a monthly magazine. He gave it to Mama and told her to keep it to read. I was only nine when Papa died and Mama valued the poem, mentioned it to me over the years and read it to me occasionally.

I thought about the poem some time ago when reading a story about a musician who played keyboard and sang in a Starbucks shop near Times Square in New York. It was a cold day so a large group had crowded inside the shop to enjoy the warmth and the music. It was a fun time and was beginning to be a profitable day for the musician as his basket for tips kept piling up.

The music was mostly from the 40s to the 90s with a few original tunes thrown in. During an emotional rendition of the classic, "If You Don't Know Me by Now," the musician noticed a lady sitting nearby singing along with him and swaying to the beat.

After the tune was over, she walked over and said, "I apologize for singing along on that song. Did it bother you?"

"No," the musician told her. "We love it when the audience joins in!" Then he added, "Would you like to sing up front on the next selection?"

She accepted his invitation. She was told to choose a song and was then asked, "What are you in the mood to sing?"

Finally she asked, "Do you know any hymns?"

He replied; "Hymns, sure? I cut my teeth on hymns. Before I was even born, I was going to church." Then he added, "How about *His Eye is on the Sparrow*?"

The lady was silent for a minute but then told him, "OK, let's do *His Eye is on the Sparrow*."

She slowly put down her purse, straightened her jacket and faced the center of the shop and began to sing:

> *Why should I be discouraged?*
> *Why should the shadows come?*

The audience of coffee drinkers was transfixed. Even the noises of the cappuccino machine ceased as the employees stopped what they were doing to listen. The song rose to its conclusion:

> *I sing because I'm happy;*
> *I sing because I'm free*
> *His eye is on the sparrow*
> *And I know He watches me.*

The applause crescendoed to a roar and continued while the musician embraced his new friend and told her she had made his day. She told him, "Well, it's funny that you picked that particular hymn."

"Why is that?" he asked.

"Well," she hesitated again, "That was my daughter's favorite song. She died at age 16 with a brain tumor two days ago." She smiled through tear-filled eyes as the musician hugged her. She said, "I am going to be okay. I've just got to keep trusting the Lord and singing God's song." She picked up her bag, gave the musician her card, and then she was gone.

My mother sang *His Eye is on the Sparrow* and other hymns in the kitchen as she prepared meals and cleaned the house. Her loud and happy singing in the kitchen sometimes embarrassed me as a teenager when I would have friends over. Today it is one of my happier memories.

The man ended his story by saying, "When you get to your wit's end, you'll find God lives there."

Those were the words my Father told Mama. When she died at age 88, the hand-written poem was still in her box of keepsakes. The poem is in her handwriting and now with my keepsakes. She must have copied from a dog-eyed printed copy from the church newspaper.

Wit's End Corner

Are you standing at "Wit's End Corner"
Friend with troubled brow?
Are you thinking of what is before you
And all you are bearing now?

Does all the world seem against you,
And you in the battle alone?
Remember - at "Wit's End Corner"
Is just where God's power is shown.

Are you standing at "Wit's End Corner"
Blinded with wearying pain,
Feeling you cannot endure it,
You cannot bear the strain,

Bruised through the constant suffering,
Dizzy, and dazed, and numb?
Remember - at "Wit's End Corner"
Is where Jesus loves to come.

Are you standing at "Wit's End Corner"?
Your work before you spread,
A mountain of tasks unfinished,
And pressing on heart and head,

     Ruth Baird Shaw

Longing for strength to do it,
Stretching out trembling hands?
Remember - at "Wit's End Corner"
The burden-bearer stands.

Are you standing at "Wit's End Corner"?
Then you're just in the very spot
To learn the wondrous resources
Of Him who faileth not.

No doubt to a brighter pathway
Your footsteps will soon be moved,
But only at "Wit's End Corner"
Is the "God who is able" proved.

~Antoinette Wilson~

Meaning of "wits' end": Perplexed: unable to think what to do.

Origin: From the Bible, Psalms 107:27 - *They reel to and fro, and stagger like a drunken man, and are at their wits' end.*

A Woman's Work is Never Done

I have had a love of writing and have enjoyed writing rhymes since childhood. But like other wives and mothers, most of my time was spent in other activities. This poem, like several others, was written "tongue in cheek" and while I was the busy mother of small children. However, other mothers tell me they identify with it.

That poem that came. . . into my heart.
Unexpected. . . like a dart

I want to polish. . . For discerning…
To write it down. . . Oh, the yearning.

First, I must polish. . . Something more.
That spot from off. . . the kitchen floor

What did I write. . . A note that said,
"Excuse my child. . . He's sick in bed.

I also write. . . some words to note:
Call the dentist. . . Hem brown coat,

Wash blue sweater. . . Start the roast,
Toss a salad. . . Buy bread for toast.

Wash the dishes. . . fold the clothes,
Sew a blouse. . . Buy ribbon bows

Make a poster. . . Draw a fish,
Prepare another. . . covered dish.

Wash the windows. . . Doors and sill,
Grab the telephone. . . pay the bills.

Buy quick oatmeal. . . Cream of wheat,
Call repair man. . . mend a sheet.

Set the table. . . Kiss a hurt
Iron a tablecloth. . . Blouse and skirt,

And other chores. . . I list and / or do.
Just little things. . . the whole day through

So I continue. . . Blowing noses
And postpone things. . .Like Grandma Moses

But thank you, God. . .You did your part,
God placed a poem. . . Within my heart.

~Ruth Baird Shaw, 1973~

If You Marry Them, You Have to Kiss Them

Labor Day has been the chosen day for our Baird/Dick Family Reunion for many years and the event has been hosted numerous times at my home here in Northwest Georgia.

My home is a sprawling ranch style house with a large family room that has a long camp meeting table with benches. That's in addition to a large living room. A fireplace between the two rooms makes it possible for everyone to enjoy looking through the fireplace from one room into the other.

We also have a dining room large enough for the dining table to expand to seat twelve to fourteen people. There's a separate breakfast room with a round table for six.

After setting up a long folding table and chairs in the living room, we can comfortably seat the 45 to 50 people who attend.

But that is another story. I want to relate a story about two of my great grandchildren who were here two days before the 2007 Family Reunion.

My granddaughter, Larisa, drove Carol, her mother, down from Tennessee on Friday so Carol could help me get ready for the party. So I was happy to have them and Larisa's daughters, Lily and Sophie, here for a few days.

My daughter Deborah (who incidentally has a Masters in Early Childhood Education) loves children. She is very involved with all the children in the family and in our church and goes out of her way to make each child feel special and loved.

Deborah offered to take Lily and Sophie for a long walk while we were making preparations for the party. She decided to walk them over to the home of a dear friend in the neighborhood where there was a swing and slide set. They had a great afternoon of play.

As they were walking home, Deborah asked Lily (age 6 at the time) and Sophie (age 4), "Did you know that when your Grandma Carol and I were little, we were sisters like you two?"

Obviously the girls hadn't considered that. "Did you live in the same house?" asked Lily.

"Yes, we lived in the same house, with Grandma Ruth and her husband, your Great-GrandShaw. Then your Grandma Carol grew up and married your Papa. And I grew up and married your Uncle Gregg."

"I don't think I want to get married," volunteered Lily.

"Well, I'm not going to kiss anyone!" declared Sophie.

"If you marry them, you have to kiss them," Lily matter-of-factly informed her.

At that point, a car came down the street and the girls quickly got up on the grass in the nearest yard - something they had been careful to do - and the subject changed. Too bad!

The Relatives Came

My oldest grandchild, Lyn, the mother of three and a teacher, was at our annual family gathering on the Second Day of Christmas. Our large extended family (numbering more than 50) has celebrated Christmas together on December 26 for over 20 years. This allows for individual family or "other family" gatherings on Christmas Eve and Christmas Day.

Lyn is a thoughtful gift buyer. Among other gifts she gave me that year was a book entitled **The Relatives Came** by Cynthia Rylant. I have read and looked at the pictures - twice!

Lyn tells me that it is a book she reads to her students every year. She tells me that she gave me the book because it reminds her (and me) of all the "hugging, eating and breathing" of our big, loving, supportive and fun-loving family.

It may have been just the book I needed to read. I was tired and considering whether or not all the cooking, cleaning and emotion involved in preparing for such a large family celebration was worth it. Was it worth it to my children and grandchildren to drive across the state and some across several states to get here?

Clearly, it is a great occasion for all the young children who take turns being Santa Claus and handing out simple gifts. It is "worth any trouble" to see the little children who love to play together with siblings and cousins on the lawn or in the "children's bedroom" in the house here.

More importantly, "when the relatives come" I am always reminded of the significance of these gatherings where family ties are renewed and wonderful times of one-on-one sharing, along with group interaction, cement the bonds of family. We truly love being with each other and these times – though a lot of work to pull together – are important for all of us and we each make the effort every year.

Autumn Wisdom

The Prophet Isaiah (55:12) talks about mountains and hills breaking forth into singing and trees clapping their hands.

It seems to me the mountains are singing clearer and louder in autumn than any other season of the year. It is in the fall of the year that the mountains call us to see and hear and experience the beauty of the mountains!

John Muir made some interesting comments about trees - not just about trees singing but preaching, too! He wrote: "Few are altogether deaf to the preaching of pine trees. Their sermons on the mountains go to our hearts; and if people in general could be got into the woods, even for once, to hear the trees speak for themselves, all difficulties in the way of forest preservation would vanish." (John Muir, naturalist, explorer and writer, 1838-1914)

A dahlia blooming in a pot near my driveway
(Photo by Joan Turrentine, October 2010)

A vase of beautiful autumn blooming dahlias from the garden of Terrell and Sheila Shaw, October 17, 2009

A few years ago, Ken Cook, a meteorologist, spoke to our Retired Pastors group at Simpsonwood United Methodist Center about his flower business in North Georgia. He told us that his dahlias bloom in the spring and in the fall. He said that when they bloom again in the fall, the colors are more vibrant and sparkling than when they bloomed in the spring. "More vibrant, more sparkling in the fall!"

What about the Autumn of life? I wrote a poem! The last verse of my poem is for all of us who are "old" and for the rest of us who are planning on getting a "whole lot older."

Autumn Wisdom

I walked into October
And lifted up my ears to hear
The very mountains singing
Choir-robed for praise . . .
in Autumn . . . clear . . .

Sunset yellows, burning bush reds.
My heart . . . in awe . . . took off its shoes

And stood on Holy ground to view
Creation's God in Autumn hue . . .

For every tree was clapping
The Doxology . . . lifted high
I think some unseen maestro
Was pointing to the sky!

I heard the mountains singing
With concert voices raised
When every hill pulled out the stops,
Adorned in breathless Autumn praise!.

I shall long remember this:
The mountains grandest notes are sung
Not in springtime's newness .
But in autumn's aging tongue.

~Ruth Baird Shaw, 1989~

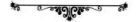

Thirteen Things about Me

My niece, Jane Lathem, who had a blog named **Cozy Reader**, posted "Thirteen Things about Me" in which she wrote thirteen things people might not know about her. She challenged me to do the same. Here are my thirteen:

1. As a child, I was afraid of the dark. I still do not like to sleep in complete darkness. As far as I know there were no nightlights in the 30s, but a small kitchen light burned all night at our home. My mother said that before electricity, she always burned a lamp with the wick turned low at night. Mama said she started doing that when she had small babies that required feedings and diaper changes in the night.

2. I was painfully shy when I was a child. I am still an introvert, but I finally overcame shyness by seeing it as self-consciousness - the emphasis being on "self." Thus, it is related to selfishness and sinfulness. "Sin" can be defined as anything that hurts or damages a person and thus something one needs to dismiss from one's life.

3. I like to write. Did I mention that I am also a philosopher, or a person given to philosophizing? My writing and poems tend to contain bits of my values and beliefs on two important things in life — faith and family. Also I have liked to write and have written "poems" since early childhood.

---

4. Like Jane...I have never eaten sushi!

5. The siblings nearest my age were three brothers. My youngest brother was five years older than I, and he played mostly with our brothers. So I, as the youngest daughter and the youngest child of nine, was virtually raised like an only child. Translation: SPOILED!

6. My closest brush with celebrity was with Guy Sharp. Guy was music director and choir leader at Park Street United Methodist Church. He and his wife, Virginia, were both talented soloists and in church with us the four years we were at Park Street (1975-1979). They remained life-long friends. Guy came over to College Park and sang a solo at the funeral service for Charles in 1986. Guy Sharpe, as all Georgians know, was a well-known and popular Atlanta weatherman and television personality. Guy was, in fact, offered the opportunity to go national as a TV weatherman while we were with him at Park Street, but he chose to stay in Atlanta.

7. I was interviewed and asked questions about the East Point Avenue church ministry on an Atlanta television program in 1993 during the four years while I was pastor of East Point Avenue United Methodist Church.

8. I once broke both arms! I fell backward, getting tangled up in a vacuum cleaner cord. As a result, I spent 6 weeks with one arm in a cast and the other arm in a splint. Fortunately my husband was still living. As one can imagine, when he was home, we became very close! He even went to the bathroom with me and one day put curlers in my hair after shampooing it. That was a riot but fun!

9. My feet grew one size with each of my first 4 pregnancies. I started out wearing a 6 ½ and I went to a 7 with my first pregnancy and to a 7 ½ with the second. Fortunately my feet did not continue growing with every child at that rate. I

ended up with seven children and now wear a size 8 ½ shoe.

10. I had a different doctor with each of my seven pregnancies - not by choice (theirs or mine) but because of several moves.

11. My singing voice is good. It is a family thing. One of the most welcomed compliments I ever received, and I gladly relate here, is that the music director at Grantville UM Church said my voice range was perfect! She encouraged me to sing solos while I was pastor there, but I did not continue. So you have to take my word for it. I did sing in the Candler Choral in seminary! Does that count?

12. I went back to school after my children were grown and earned a Bachelor's and a Master's degree after age sixty. I aged into the study of Gerontology and was also certified in Gerontology at Georgia State University.

13. I am a preacher! The last thing I ever wanted to be or expected to be was a preacher. I have been a Christian believer as far back as I remember. I had a definite conversion experience and decision at the age of eleven. For a long time I postponed the call to preach that both my husband and I recognized as early as 1975. But I am a woman. All woman! I was reluctant to take on the enmity.

But one awesome day in 1986, the Lord opened a door and pushed me into the pulpit and into Christian ministry. God has enabled me to do, and to do well, the task the Lord called me to do! I run to the task, rejoice and accept every opportunity to speak and have never tired of telling the story of God's amazing love and grace!

Ruth Baird Shaw

I'm Fixing to Get My Hair Fixed

My daughter, Carol, a school teacher, called on the way to school early one morning. In the course of the conversation she asked about my day. I told her I had an appointment at 11:00 to "get my hair fixed." Carol, a Southern girl, did not laugh at my choice of words. She understood what I meant.

Later in the morning, a friend, Ann Short, called and said, "Whatcha doing?" I told Ann I was about to go out the door to "get my hair fixed." Ann did not laugh, either. When I ended the second conversation, I laughed! In fact I laughed out loud even though I was home alone. Can we really "fix" our hair? Does it become broken? Well, it does sometimes need "repair."

Earlier this week, we had a family marathon of indignant emails. "How discourteous," we wrote, "for anyone to laugh in our faces at our choice of words or speech!" It all started when one family member wrote, "I had to work hard to quit saying 'show out' when I got ribbed mercilessly about my choice of words while living 'up North.'"

"Have you ever thought," we asked one another, "how interesting it is that people in the South are 'ribbed mercilessly' for our language choices, and it seems to have never occurred to anyone from the South to 'rib mercilessly' people in other parts of our great United States of America for the many strange phrases they use in their speech?"

We had fun emailing back and forth arrogantly telling each other how "arrogant" our Northern brothers and sisters are to laugh at our speech patterns and turning the tables by laughing at their speech with such statements as "I have heard that a New York accent is the best birth control there is."

But, where in the world did we ever get the phrase "I'm fixing to get my hair fixed"?

The Exploitation of Children

The first news I heard very early this morning was beyond the imagination of normal adults in a civilized country: the arrests and breaking up of a pedophilia molestation ring on the internet. Children, one as young as eighteen months, were being brutally assaulted and sexually molested.

Back about 1988, my brother, a cousin and I drove down to Griffin, Georgia to attend the funeral of a cousin. Our conversation turned to family history. My mother's family was not wealthy but produced community leaders, teachers, preachers, land owners, and office holders.

My mother's young father died of pneumonia when she was 18 months old and when her mother was pregnant with their eighth child. She grew up in a little house on her grandfather's farm. Her grandfather was a community and church leader. He was a respected Methodist preacher and owned a large farm. But this was in the late 19th century. The South was still in reconstruction. Times were bad. Many who still owned land were "land poor." Later some of the children had to drop out of school and work in the cotton fields, and some of the children took jobs in a cotton mill nearby to help support their widowed mother and siblings.

So on this trip to Griffin, my older brother, Bill (eighteen years older than I), recounted to me some of the family history. Our conversation turned to talking about how wonderful it was now to have better opportunities for women left alone with children. Now widows had more opportunities; child labor laws meant children no longer leave school to work in cotton fields and mills to help support their families.

Then I thought, in some respects, we have gone backwards. We do not have children slaving away in cotton fields or standing on stools to reach spindles in cotton mills, but we have child alcoholics and child drug addicts. There are children who are abused emotionally, physically and sexually. Some children are so troubled they end up stealing and killing. You know the headlines as well as I.

There is an answer, and it is God's answer. During those difficult years, many learned about God's love and wonderful plan for life. In desperation, many believed and turned to God's plan by faith in Jesus Christ.

In our prosperity, our children were able to go back to school, be educated, and get good jobs or have good careers. Then, in our arrogance, many said, "OK, God, we'll take over now."

How much more tragedy - how many more ruined lives do we have to see - before we, as individuals and as a nation, wake up.

The Wilberforce Signing

On the evening of December 10, 2008, the **William Wilberforce Trafficking Victims Protection Act** was passed by both houses of Congress. The White House invited ten representatives from non-government organizations to be present at the Wilberforce signing in the Oval Office. They also invited 4 political appointees in various offices that deal with anti-trafficking efforts.

Pictured above is our daughter, Dr. Janice Crouse, who was one of those chosen for this historical signing in the Oval office (Janice is on President George W. Bush's left). The Wilberforce signing was part of the battle to pass the **William Wilberforce Trafficking Victims Protection Act**.[5]

---

[5] Other invited quests for the signing in the picture above include L to R, Michael Chertoff- former Secretary of Homeland Security, Michael Horowitz -Hudson Institute, Rachel Lloyd - Girls Educational and Mentoring Services (GEMS), NYC, Gary Haugen - International Justice Mission, Brad Miles - Polarius Project, Kevin Bales - Author of **Disposal People**. Directly behind Janice Shaw Crouse is Richard Land, head of Ethics and Religious Liberty Commission for Southern Baptists.

Those chosen for the signing were people who have worked on the front lines of the policy battles over the anti-trafficking efforts.

The widespread and increasing use of rape as a systematic weapon of war, even of genocide, the international trafficking in persons, mainly women and children, has also risen alarmingly. Children are sold and women are lured or kidnapped and then sold into sexual slavery.

William Wilberforce, 1759-1833

William Wilberforce came from a prosperous merchant family of Kingston-upon-Hull, a North Sea port. At twenty-one, he was elected to Parliament for his native town. A conversion to evangelical Christianity in 1785 changed his approach to politics. In 1787 he became the parliamentary leader of the slavery abolition movement. William Wilberforce labored ceaselessly for the abolition of slavery.

John Wesley, on the 24th of February, 1793 at age eighty-eight, and a week before his death, wrote the last letter he would ever write. The letter was to Wilberforce, urging him to continue the fight for the abolition of slavery. Wesley wrote, "...Oh, be not weary in well-doing. Go on, in the name of God and in the power of His might, till slavery, the vilest that ever saw the sun, shall be banished away."

My Song of Praise

Just a year or so before my husband, Charles, had his first heart attack, we were pulling off the expressway to go to our United Methodist parsonage in Austell where we lived at the time.

We saw a man fall down beside the road. We had gone past him so we had to get to a place to turn around and drive back. Charles asked me to stay in the car until he talked to the man. The man was on crutches with a broken leg in a cast and was falling down drunk.

Charles put him in the car, took him home with us, put him in the shower and helped him get a bath while I washed his clothes and prepared him something to eat. Later Charles was able to get him into a Christian home for alcoholics.

So it is. We come to Jesus just as we are, clothed in the garments of sin, spiritually starving and sick unto death. We are welcomed by Christ (and hopefully by Christians), accepted just as we are, bathed in God's love and forgiveness - transformed and clothed in his Grace - indeed given a place at His table of Grace.

I heard Dottie Rambo tell of praying for a brother who had become alcoholic. He was finally won to the Lord and was the inspiration of one of my favorites of all of Dottie's songs.

He Looked Beyond My Faults and Saw My Need

Amazing Grace shall always be my song of praise
For it was Grace that bought my liberty
I do not know just why He came to love me so
He looked beyond my fault and saw my need

I shall forever lift mine eyes to Calvary.
To view the cross where Jesus died for me
How marvelous…the Grace that caught my falling soul
He looked beyond my fault and saw my need

Trigeminal Neuralgia

I had never heard of trigeminal neuralgia until I was diagnosed with it. Below is a brief history of my bout with trigeminal neuralgia which will be of interest and hopefully helpful to many other TN sufferers out there. I am writing about my experience because other TN sufferers have called to ask and I wish someone had given me information early on. It might have helped in some of the decisions I made for treatment.

My first attack of TN was in August of 1990. I was in my sixties and had never heard of trigeminal neuralgia. I was to learn this is not unusual. Many patients have suffered for years, going from one doctor to another, before being diagnosed with TN.

At first, the acute "electric shock" type of pain seemed localized in my teeth. I went to a dentist. I had an unnecessary root canal before they discovered that wasn't the problem. The dentist was not 100% sure it was not that bottom left jaw tooth. When the unbearable pain continued, the dentist ruled out my teeth as the problem.

Finally a doctor, after finding no brain tumor or other problems that could cause such horrible pain, diagnosed it as trigeminal neuralgia.

The neurologist I saw at the time seemed to have had little or no experience with TN. Six years after my first attack, after six years of excruciating pain attacks, on March 6, 1996, Dr. Susie Tindall at Emory University Hospital in Atlanta did brain surgery - micro vascular decompression. In lay person's understanding, a pad was placed to separate the offending trigeminal nerve from the artery pulsating against it. Dr. Tindall had told me it was "successful in 80 percent of patients."

After the surgery Dr. Tindall told my family that it "did not look like what she expected." My understanding is she did not see an artery pulsating against a nerve but she put a pad in anyway. The surgery was not successful so the horrible pain started up again after a brief time. One of the frustrations about TN is the intermittent pain that comes and goes without apparent cause or reason.

After moving to Rome, Georgia in 1998, my pain kept increasing. My son-in-law, Gregg Lewis, a writer, had just written a book with Dr. Benjamin Carson. Gregg knew that Carson, the director of pediatric neurosurgery at Johns Hopkins, also specialized in TN treatments for adults.

On June 10, 1999, I went to Johns Hopkins Medical Center in Baltimore, Maryland for Dr. Carson to do a procedure labeled "Percutaneous trigeminal rhizotomy with glycerin injection." My pain continued.

Later I learned from Patricia Sumerford of Big Canoe, Georgia about a support group she was starting for trigeminal sufferers. A friend, Ann Long, of Grantville, Georgia, at a meeting happened to overhear Patricia mention TN, and she gave her my e-mail address. Patricia was most helpful and gave me information about a research project taking place at Life University in Marietta under the direction of Dr. Roger Hinson, a Chiropractic doctor.

I got in touch with Dr. Hinson and participated in the project for nearly a year and was pleased with my progress. While I was getting chiropractic adjustments from Dr. Hinson, I gradually reduced the amount of the Neurontin I was taking and got off medication completely for a while and was practically pain free.

After the research, when I stopped making the long trip down to Marietta, the breathtaking electric shock like pain came back and became increasingly severe. I tried a chiropractic doctor here in Rome but continued in severe pain. The indescribable pain became more and more severe.

Dr. Hinson is in private practice now in College Park, Georgia. I am told that medical insurance will now cover some chiropractic treatments. I continued seeing a neurologist, Dr. Bill Naguazewski, who kept increasing my Neurontin - a medicine commonly used in epilepsy patients - and they even put a pain patch on me one day when I was at the doctor's office in such horrible pain I could not speak. I got off the narcotic pain patch after a few weeks believing the treatment was worse than the disease.

Medication - even pain patches - does not help this pain anyway, and I certainly did not want to deal with addictive drugs.

The doctors did CT scans which showed that the pad that Dr. Tindall put in my brain in the 1996 surgery at Emory had calcified. The neurosurgeons here in Rome were helpless. They said they had never seen anything like it.

We finally sent the scans to a neurosurgeon in Nashville and then on to Johns Hopkins hospital in Baltimore. Both these doctors had seen the calcification before and both suggested another rhizotomy that would deaden the trigeminal nerve. My family did a great deal of research and finally convinced me to go back to Dr. Carson at Johns Hopkins. They reasoned Carson would have a special interest in me because of the previous failed procedure.

October 30, 2001, I was back at Johns Hopkins. Dr. Benjamin Carson did a "Rhizotomy with a modified form of radiofrequency." This is not considered a permanent solution, but it is expected to last for years - and is still working well for me years later. One of the side effects is that I have a great deal of numbness (especially the left nostril) and still have some head and facial pain but no recurrence of the unbearable trigeminal pain.

Even with the subsequent side effects, I would have the surgery again because the pain had become so unbearable. I could not eat and could not talk without extreme pain and it made carrying on daily activities difficult.

Weeding Lily's Garden!

On December 1, in 2008, the frightening word "Leukemia" swept through our family. My beautiful great-grand-daughter, Lily Hensiek, at age seven was diagnosed with Pre-B ALL (Acute Lymphocytic Leukemia).

Lily, six weeks before being diagnosed with leukemia

Lily has learned a lot since the picture on the left was taken, as has her parents and her grandparents, (my daughter Carol and her husband Ron) and especially her younger sister, Sophie, who was 5 at the time.

Lily's mother, Larisa, has handled the trauma connected with the difficult treatments with amazing strength and skill. She has been the major force behind raising close to a half million to fund research to find a cure for childhood cancer.

We have all learned about the need for more awareness and more funds to be raised to fight Childhood cancer. Until our precious Lily was diagnosed, I had no idea about the large number of children who have died and many others who have suffered from childhood cancer.

Lily's doctor explained leukemia by telling her that the leukemia cells are

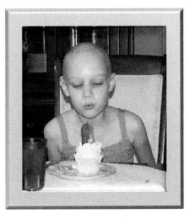

Celebrating her 8th birthday four months into treatment that would last over 2 years

like weeds that crowd out the good flowers in a garden. Lily has passed important milestones in her treatments in order to kill all the weeds so that only healthy and beautiful flowers will grow in "Lily's Garden."

Lily has emerged as a beautiful healthy and happy ten-year old. She is perhaps more serious for all the painful treatments she has endured as well as the trauma of meeting and grieving the death of many of the children she met during her treatments.

Breastfeeding

Awhile back, I read in the headline news that Actress Salma Hayak's daughter, Valentina Paloma, turned one year old in September 2008. Like other mothers before her, Hayak was reluctant to give up breastfeeding as Valentina was thriving so beautifully.

Many mothers have learned, as I learned when I was breastfeeding my first baby, that it is good to wait until the baby can drink from a cup, rather than to wean him/her to a bottle from her/his mother's milk and then from the bottle to a cup.

As most of us have been taught, there are very good reasons to breastfeed: nutrition, bonding and economics, just to name a few. And importantly, we remember that the first milk in the breast, colostrum, is the medication and nutrition the newborn baby needs.

Salma Hayek, a spokesperson for UNICEF, discovered another good reason to keep her breast milk flowing during her visit to Sierra Leone in September 2008.

In an effort to encourage West African women to breastfeed, the actress/humanitarian offered a sick baby boy the greatest gift of all - milk from her own breast. After she fed the baby, it was suggested that Hayek had been disloyal to her own baby by sharing her milk. Hayek, though, decided that she had done something good for both babies.

"My baby would be very proud to be able to share her milk," she said.

It seems that Hayek's unselfish giving of her breast milk is a bit of a family tradition. She tells the story of her own great-grandmother breastfeeding a stranger's hungry child on a street in Mexico. It's a beautiful story made more so by Hayek's own gift to a hungry little baby.

The question asked at the end of the story was: If you ever found yourself in a position to do so, would you breastfeed another woman's child? Would you allow your child to feed at another woman's breast? My answer is "yes" to both questions. Of course I would!

This story reminded me of a story in my own life I had not thought about for a long time. My sister-in-law, Ruth Mitchem Baird, and I were pregnant at the same time. My daughter, Janice, was born on June 3rd and her daughter, Gail, was born on June 14th of the same year.

One day three-month-old Janice and I were visiting my mother while my mother was babysitting Gail for my sister-in-law who had a doctor's appointment. For some reason Ruth was delayed past Gail's regular meal time. When Gail began to let us know it was getting past her dinner time, Mama turned to me and said, "You can feed her."

I was young and frankly shocked and looked at my Mother questioningly. "Sure, it is alright and a good thing to do," my wise mother assured me. So I breastfed my niece Gail and still had plenty of milk for Janice's next feeding.

Skin Cancer Surgery

In recent years I have often reflected that one of the benefits of getting old is that our eyesight dims so we cannot see all our blemishes and wrinkles. Then a few months ago I had cataract surgery and was absolutely shocked at how I had aged overnight.

After a partial adjustment to senior citizenship, a couple of little blemishes appeared on my once-beautiful face. Beautiful? My teen-aged bridegroom told me so on our wedding day, wrote beautiful love letters declaring the same for the two years he served as a Marine in World War II and kept up the same line down to his fatal heart attack forty-seven years after our wedding day. This member of The Greatest Generation knew how to talk to a woman. God bless his memory! Let me add, my husband did not claim to be, nor was he a saint. And he soon knew for sure his bride was not always "beautiful" in appearance or behavior.

Yesterday, as I lay on my back at Emory Clinic with two doctors carving on my face, one of the doctors said, "I hope you have a good story ready to explain how you got this black eye." The only black-eye story I have heard is a man explaining to his co-workers, "It is my wife and my firewood, so it is none of your business."

Forgive me, dear feminist friends. How far we have come! Only my generation of women would dare to repeat the story above, and I certainly would not tell it publicly and appear to condone violence against women. So I need the help of anyone still reading. Does anyone out there know a better story about black eyes that I can tell in church Sunday morning?

Ruth Baird Shaw

News Flash: Current Health Report

I always wanted a secretary. All the years I was serving pastorates in Grantville and East Point Avenue, I wanted a secretary. This week I've had two secretaries. My daughter, Joan, was my secretary for my Veterans Day post, and I'm dictating to my daughter, Carol, to let you know that I'm better today as I recuperate from maxillary sinus surgery of the right side of my face.

I still have a droopy eyelid and my face and lips are still quite swollen, but I definitely look better; so I'm not getting much sympathy. It still bothers me to put on my glasses, and I don't see very well. So it's nice to have my secretaries.

My health is improving every day. My right eye actually opens now, my voice sounds normal again, and the swelling is going down. I had hoped the surgeon would do a little plastic surgery and make me look better and younger. Unfortunately, I'm afraid I look older and grayer. I'm happy to be alive after that amazing surgery. I appreciate all the tender loving care and the prayers and cards and thoughts of so many family and friends.

My spirits were boosted when I got a really nice note from Galen and Brenda Foster with a picture of our house on 97 Elm Street in Milstead. That's the house we bought when Charles came home from World War II. We lived next door to Charles's Marine buddy, Grover Foster, Galen's dad.

Grover's wife, Myrl, and I became good friends and were pregnant at the same time. Terry and Galen were both born in March of 1947 and played together, had their own language and chatted with each other. It was so cute. They remained good friends until we moved a few years later.

As I've said before, one of the benefits of growing older is having wonderful memories of previous years to cherish and enjoy in old age.

Remember and Re-member

I went back to school after my children were grown so aged into the study of aging. While working on my degree at Georgia State University, I also earned a certificate in Gerontology and did an internship at a large complex for elderly and disabled people.[6]

During the course of the time I was at the convalescent center, I taught a poetry class to a group of elderly patients on Saturday mornings for six weeks. Some of the elderly patients had arthritic fingers and had difficulty holding a pencil. So I would have them tell me their poem - something about their life, an event, a memory - and I would write it down in poetic form and read it back to them and to the group.

I learned much from these elderly citizens. I especially remember an elderly nurse, Rose, telling her poem of how when her mother called all the children in for supper, she was always the child "sitting on the highest limb...of the tallest tree." When I read Rose's poem to her cohorts in nurse care, her wrinkled face lit up with joy as she relived this remembering.

Mr. Roberts, an elderly man in a wheelchair, told me his poem. He recounted:

> *Everything was not good*
> *In the good old days.*
> *Everything was not safe*
> *In the good old days.*

---

[6] This large "Christian City" complex included individual homes for elderly or disabled couples or individuals, a convalescent center, a nursing care building and an Alzheimer's unit.

One day when I,
Was about knee high.
Not more than four years old.
I took a stick of dynamite
Out to the railroad track.
My father used dynamite
To clear his land for plowing.
Dynamite made a loud noise!
I wanted to make it
Make a loud noise!
My mother looked out and saw me.
My mother trembled
As she came to get me.
My mother was afraid to call me.
My mother's hands trembled
As she reached out to me
And took the dynamite!

As I read Mr. Roberts' poem back to him and to the group, no longer did I see only an elderly man in a wheelchair. I also envisioned a small, precocious boy, a child who had loving parents; a father he wanted to emulate and a mother who would risk her very life to protect him.

By remembering…by the gift of memory, this disabled and elderly man was a young child again, remembering who he was. He was somebody. He was loved!

Probably in Mr. Roberts' early memories he thought primarily of the danger he had encountered in this childhood escapade. Now, elderly and disabled, the smiling Mr. Roberts was remembering a strong daddy who worked hard to support him and a young mother's love for him and her bravery on his account. This gave him added status in his own eyes and in the eyes of his neighbors in the nursing home who were now hearing his story. He may have been an old man in a wheelchair, but he was thus able to tell something of his story to others around him. He remembered who he was. He was thus able to share his story.

One sociologist has suggested that we hyphenate the term re-member to distinguish it from ordinary recollection or reminiscing. Re-membering is the reconstructing of one's members. It is the reconstructing of the figures that properly belong to one's prior selves. Through re-membering, a life is given shape and form and extends back into the past and forward into the future as an edited story. Through re-membering our entire life is put in perspective. Without re-membering we lose our history and ourselves.

Good news! When we read the Bible, we realize the Lord God knew about the importance of remembering long before the sociologists found out about it! All the way back to the book of Deuteronomy, the God of Israel, the God that Jesus called "Father," kept telling the descendants of Israel to remember. "And you shall remember all the ways which the Lord your God has led you these forty years in the wilderness, that God might humble you, testing you to know what was in your heart, whether you would keep God's commandments or not."[7]

My daughter Joan, a gifted teacher, tells about how schools have gone to seed in teaching children "self-esteem" for "smiles' rather than from real accomplishments. Her experiences with children in school have convinced her that, while children certainly need positive reinforcement and personal attention, they learn self-esteem primarily from remembering their work done well.[8]

Re-membering is not the same as reminiscing. I learned in working with the elderly that there is a difference in the people who just recollect things about their past and those who re-member.

In other words the people of God were to begin their worship liturgy with a recitation of remembrance. Re-membering, giving shape and form to all their story which included those who had gone before them as well as the God who had lead them. The Hebrew people in the Bible were to understand who they were. It

---

[7] Deuteronomy 26
[8] Daddy's Roses blog by Joan Shaw Turrentine

began with Abraham, a wandering Armenian, who had believed in the promises of God.[9]

We read about God telling Abram his descendants would be numerous as the stars, and he and Sarah were already elderly and childless and the Bible tells us Abram believed God and it was put into his account as righteousness![10]

So here we see his descendants standing in the door of the Promised Land with their first-fruits in their hand. They are recounting their story and it is also God's story! It's a beautiful liturgy of re-membering. "A wandering Armenian was my father and we had bad times. In fact, we were afflicted. We were oppressed. But we have a God. And God acted on our behalf! We are no longer a "no people" We are God's people!"

[9] Deuteronomy 8:2
[10] Genesis 15:1-12, 17, 18a

One Sunday Morning

My husband, Charles Shaw, had been a pastor in the Methodist Church for thirty five years when he had a second heart attack which left him with heart damage. He had to retire from his work as a full time pastor.

About a year later, Rev. Harold Gray, the District Superintendent (an Elder who helps with seeing that each church in his district has a pastor) called one Sunday morning and asked Charles if he would go preach at a small United Methodist Church whose preacher could not continue.

Charles and I drove the 22 miles to the beautiful Rico UMC in Palmetto, Georgia where less than a dozen people were present, not knowing whether or not they would have a pastor to lead the service.

Neither the church nor the Bishop ever sought a replacement, and so Charles continued to serve at Rico for over a year. Attendance and membership grew with Charles as their gifted preacher and loving pastor.

Two of those Sundays Charles asked me to preach when he was not able. The First Sunday in Advent in 1986, Charles preached his last sermon, suffering a fatal heart attack three days later.

Two weeks after my husband's death, I learned the Rico congregation had made a request to the church cabinet that I be appointed as their pastor. So I stood there to preach my first sermon as a pastor only three Sundays after my husband had stood in that same pulpit to preach his last.

Even though I had been on the periphery of ministry a long time, the role of pastor was a new one! When I was asked to take on the pastorate, I was surprised that they would call a woman pastor. However, I knew I would continue in ministry in some way as long as I lived because of my strong sense of calling, and I knew this was the open door the Lord wanted me to walk through!

The Lord blessed us richly as I continued to serve the Lord in that place for nearly four years while enrolling in and finishing seminary.

The Rico United Methodist Church is located in the beautiful open countryside and is only a hundred yards or so from the Providence Baptist Church. When I first went to Rico, I was interested to learn that the Baptist and Methodist congregations join together for worship services at least three times a year and also cooperate with each other in other ways.

The Rico United Methodist Church

For example, each has an annual homecoming and both congregations come together for the fellowship dinner after the Worship Service. They attend each other's weddings and "showers." Why so much fellowship across denominational lines? When I read the Rico Church History I found at least one answer.

In 1902 when a man by the name of Shannon gave an acre of land adjoining the new Baptist church to build the Methodist Church he said, "The Baptist and Methodists should cooperate on earth as well as in heaven." Then in 1954 in an updated history this story is re-told with the comment, "It is said that there is no place on earth where Methodists and Baptists cooperate more than in the Rico Community." So, at least for the old timers in the area, they took pride, perhaps even "un-Christian pride" in recounting their history of cooperation.

One of the joint ventures is a service at the Masonic Hall on the third Sunday of each September. I have not polled "the whole world" but I suspect there may be no other place on earth where Baptists and Methodists unite for a Sunday Worship Service in a Masonic Hall.

This includes the two pastors preaching in alternating years. The Masonic Lodge is equidistant from the two churches, in a triangle with the three buildings near one point on the triangle. The Masonic structure is a little nearer the Methodist than the Baptist, a fact that I understood was pleasing to some of the Baptists who considered the Masonic movement a work of the devil.

It was my turn to preach. I had been a pastor less than a year and was a student in seminary. I had put all the time I could in preparation and felt it was not nearly enough. The Baptist preacher would lead the singing and the pastoral prayer. After Sunday school both congregations walked the few yards to gather for this service. All of our Methodist people were present.

One family had even postponed a vacation in order to "support Ruth" in my first attempt to preach to the Baptists. Some of the Baptist members chose to go home or somewhere else. We had about an equal number from each of the two congregations. They were seated in clusters in what could be described as a "theater-in-the-round." I do not know if this arena style is typical of Masonic structures.

Rev. Glenn Dow, the Baptist minister, was seated on my left on the slightly raised stage at the wall in front of the entrance.

We were into the service and our Methodist Children's Choir was singing (Yes, we did have a Children's Choir by this time - thanks to Judy Henderson, who with her husband, Ernie, had joined Rico Church, bringing their three children and also neighborhood children). A man came to the open door and motioned for Dow. It seemed like an eternity before he returned to the platform visibly shaken. He walked to the podium and said, "I have a very sad announcement to make. I wish it could wait until after the service, but in my judgment it needs to be told now. There has been a terrible accident out on Garrett's Ferry Road. It was Charlene Lewis and her children on the way to church. The children were rushed to Grady. Charlene is dead. It is time for prayer and they need prayer. We all need prayer. Let us pray."

There were audible gasps and cries all over the building. I found myself in tears. I had met Charlene and her two young daughters just eight days earlier at a wedding shower at our Methodist church for a Baptist friend. She was young and very much alive.

The shock of sudden death is staggering. We were all reeling. My mind was in turmoil as I was bowed low listening to Dow and silently praying for the grieving congregation and for myself. What in the world could I say?

Painfully I struggled to remember some of the sermon notes folded in my Bible. Would it be appropriate? The scripture I had asked Dow to read was Paul's account in Romans 4:1-11 of Abram's life of faith and a few verses in Luke 15:3-7 about God's love for one lost sheep. I was to tie them together with the thought that God loves us and has a place and a plan for each of us. God's laws are not just written in the Bible, but are also written in our bodies and our psyche. When we come home to God we are coming home to Truth.

We did not know at the time that the only child of a neighbor had also been killed. A drunken man had driven his car on the wrong side of this peaceful and picturesque county road.

I do not remember Dow's prayer. I do remember thinking he was handling it well. I had and still have great respect for this man of God. His pastoral care and concern was evident. Rev. Dow finished the prayer and sat down like a man whose sentence was served and looked expectantly toward me.

It was all too soon my turn to speak. Before beginning the sermon I said a few things I had planned about my respect for the Baptist church and a few words about my call as a woman. Very few! When faced with the mystery of death, the disputes between denominational understanding and between the place of men and women in the church seemed insignificant. I could not just "be with the people." I knew if there were to be any ultimate truths to be spoken by a human being, for God's sake and for ours it must be said. I was not adequate but I knew the Eternal God was with me in a powerful way.

It was not a funeral. It was a Sunday Morning worship service. But we were crying for Charlene and for our own humanness. I said something like this; "I met Charlene at the shower for Linda last week. I remember her as vivacious and friendly." I turned to my right where several persons were sobbing. "I grieve with you. I am so sorry…so very sorry. I grieve for all of us in trying to understand how a loving, all powerful God would allow a young mother to be killed on the way to church."

"We know, of course, thousands of persons drove to church safely today but that does not make it easier. And in our humanness, we take our safety, our lives for granted. We only stop to question God when an accident or sudden death occurs."

Standing at the pulpit of Rico United Methodist Church

"God has given us freedom. We are in a highly mechanized, fallen world and it seems to me many persons' lives are cut short needlessly. I remember the lines in Isaiah 40:8: "The grass withers, the flowers fade, but the word of our God stands forever." You and I die. How I wish it were not so. How I wish things were different. But if things were different, it is entirely possible that we would not possess whatever it is…we wish would never die."

Ruth Baird Shaw

"Moses wrote in Psalm 90: 'A thousand years in God's sight are but as a day when it is past and as a watch in the night.' It seems to me that measuring the length of life in the light of eternity - whether we live a hundred years or just twenty or thirty years - we have only a brief time. This is why it is so important to learn from God. The eternal God is our dwelling place and underneath are the everlasting arms. This is why what we do at church is of supreme importance."

It was one of the most heartwarming and faith building experiences of my life to look at the sermon the Lord gave me during that week. I did not know what would be happening on that Sunday morning but it was evident the Lord did. From the opening story to the final illustration, the sermon spoke to all of us in the crisis situation in which we found ourselves that day.

Everyone stayed to complete the Celebration of Worship until the last amen of the benediction. Then they came forward in tears to put arms of love around Dow and around me and each other and to say affirming things about the service and about their faith.

Semper Fidelis: Always Faithful

In my house there is one room I use for a "study." The room holds my computer, two desks and has two walls filled to overflowing with books.

When my granddaughter, Amanda, was small, she liked to come in here and write library cards for her smaller cousins. She called this "the library." I recent years, I spend a great deal of my time in this room reading as well as writing.

Family members, including children when they visit, are welcome and usually make a least one stop to check e-mail or just "putter around" looking at pictures when they visit. The young children usually ask for and receive a supply of paper and pencil to write or draw and make themselves at home in "the library."

On my hallway wall just outside my study is a gallery of family pictures that fascinates the younger children. They love to find pictures of themselves and their parents on Grandma Ruth's wall.

Shortly before Charles died in 1986, he had framed a Semper Fidelis emblem. It now hangs near his pictures in my study.

Charles, like most Marines, was proud to be a member of the United States Marines. He served in the Marine Corps in World War II in the South Pacific. "Semper Fidelis," always faithful, was more than a motto to him and to his buddies and also to the wives and widows of these men, who do not question that they were indeed the "greatest generation."

However, my grandson, who recently returned to Germany after serving over a year in the U.S. Army in Iraq, and his generation are also struggling daily and honorably with new enemies as we finally saw clearly on September 11, 2001 after years of more minor attacks on Americans.

All of this to tell of an article I read in the newspaper recently: "Man gets 15 months for lying about Iraq video." What would make anyone hate America so much he would make false, fictitious and fraudulent statements about someone in our Armed Services?

Why would our news media broadcast the Abu Ghraib case 24 hours a days and report the unproven story about the Marine on their front pages and then place the true account on page 3?
So you may not have heard that Dellon Tyler Ward pleaded guilty months ago to two counts of "knowingly and willfully making false, fictitious and fraudulent statements" to federal agents last year. He also presented video footage which allegedly showed members of the Marine Corps "committing murder on Iraqi soil."

The investigation of these false charges ended up costing $193,000 and involved pulling U.S. Marines out of combat zones in the spring of 2007. Many people still believe his lies were truth. He received only 15 months for this treason.

The Wedding Dress

Janice was first to wear "The Dress"

In our society today, weddings are often big business. In "Dear Abby" recently, someone wrote to deplore the fact that some people spend their last dime and even go into debt to "put on a big wedding." Of course the main problem is that the wedding sometimes seems to be judged more important than the marriage.

Being the mother of five daughters and two sons, as well as the wife of a pastor, I became, out of necessity, somewhat of a specialist in planning weddings at which my husband officiated. Usually I would be invited to the rehearsal as well as the wedding. So it was often my assignment to try to calm nerves. I did that by reminding the bride and groom and mothers: "Don't worry. We are just going to get

Joan wore "The Dress" two years later

dressed up and go down to the church for a wedding ceremony. If the ring is dropped or someone makes an error, these are the human elements we like to remember, laugh about later and tell our grandchildren!"

When our oldest daughter, Janice, was about to graduate from college and was planning her wedding later in the summer, she asked a couple of friends to be in the wedding. She picked out material for the bridesmaids' dresses and sent it to the friends who were to be bridesmaids.

Carol was the third to wear it

Her younger sister, Joan, was to be maid of honor, and younger sisters, Carol, Deborah and Beth, were to be junior bridesmaids. So I had a great deal of sewing to do as well as buying suits for our two sons - one of whom was to light the candles. The youngest son was only three,

Debi was fourth in line to wear "The Dress"

I did a lot of sewing in those days and was making the 4 bridesmaid dresses and because of a real shortage of money, I was also planning to make the wedding gown.

When Janice got home from school, she and I went down to Rich's department store in Atlanta to buy fabric, and while looking at fabric I had a sudden inspiration that turned out to be an answer to prayer.

Beth was the last of our five daughters to wear "The Dress"

I said to Janice, "Let's go up to Rich's Bridal Shop and see what we would buy if money were no object and get some ideas about the

pattern and material we need to buy." When we got to the Bridal Shop, we found just exactly what we would have bought if we'd had a fat bank account - a stunningly beautiful ivory silk gown with alencon needlepoint lace, seeded pearls and a traditional train!

A wonderful thing happened. The sales lady told us the gown had been part of a bridal fashion show a day earlier. So they were marking it down to about a fourth of the original price. The beautiful gown was a perfect fit for Janice, like it had been made for her.

Vicki, David's bride, wore "The Dress" sixth

We were able to buy the gown at the new price and went home with a light heart because one of the major items in our wedding plans could be checked off the list!

The dress became something of a family heirloom. Janice wore it, and later all four of her sisters, a sister-in-law and many years later Janice's daughter, Charmaine, wore "The Dress".

A second generation: Janice's daughter, Charmaine, was the last to wear "The Dress"

Janice's Dad who was also the church's pastor escorted his first daughter down the church aisle. After "giving her away" he then officiated at the wedding. In the coming years, he would escort all five daughters down the church aisle, and he officiated at the weddings of all seven children as well.

Ruth Baird Shaw

A Letter from Camp

David reached age 11 and was excited to take his place for a week at Summer Camp in Dahlonega, the family tradition his six siblings before him had enjoyed.

As his mother, I helped him pack for the trip. I had bought him new underwear and included the new package of underwear in his luggage. I also added a self-addressed card to send to us from camp as a good exercise in writing.

Fortunately David was back home with his head still attached and still "filling good" before the card below arrived.

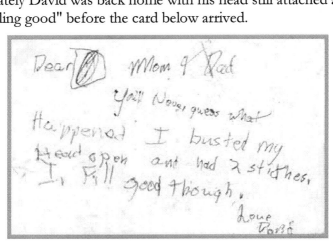

P.S. Also... his new underwear was still new in the unopened package.

The Tree Planting

"I think that I shall never see a poem as lovely as a tree..."

I thought of Joyce Kilmer's well-known poem this week when Ann Long, a friend from Grantville, sent me a photo of the Methodist parsonage in Grantville in which I lived from 1990 to 1993.

This photo shows the church as it looked in the 1990s when I lived in the wonderful little town of Grantville. I could write a book about my three years living among those beautiful people. You can see the parsonage behind the church.

Ann wanted me to see the tall tulip tree that had been only a tiny sapling when we planted it in the front yard of the house while I was pastor of the Grantville First United Methodist Church.

I used the term "we planted," but I did little more than watch that spring day when Ann Long and Kathleen Ray brought their Sunday school class of little girls to plant the tree.

Kathleen, a former missionary and talented teacher, and Ann Long came that day with hole diggers, shovels, fertilizer and a tree just the right size for primary age children to plant. The "big girls" (four to six year old Mandie Crews, Sarah Hunter, Katie Hunter, Sarah Bonner, and Cathy Smith) worked alongside toddlers, Morgan Crews and Annalee Hunter. As the tree grew, so grew the children. One memorable Sunday while there, we saw a miracle when the Grantville church family had worked with me to fill the sanctuary and the balcony to overflowing in celebration of the church's sesquicentennial - 150 years in service to God and the world.

The parsonage was a beautifully furnished and comfortable home provided for the pastoral family. We could walk out the front door of the pastor's home and walk a few feet across the road into the back door of the church building.

I could walk down the hill every early morning to pick up mail. The Post Office was a quick gathering place for all of us on our way to work. I talked with Baptist deacons who were gracious enough to welcome me to town. "Grace" does make us gracious enough to love one another even when we have different Biblical understandings of a Christian woman's place in the church.

The Grantville UMC parsonage was also conveniently located to City Hall. While I was a resident of Grantville, I walked down that hill many times to "open with prayer" the city council's monthly meetings.

I (a fool like me) have planted a few trees, but Kilmer is right that "only God can make a tree." Here is the entire poem:

Trees

I think that I shall never see
A poem as lovely as a tree.
A tree whose hungry mouth is pressed
Against the earth's sweet flowing breast;
A tree that looks at God all day,
And lifts her leafy arms to pray;

A tree that may in Summer wear

A nest of robins in her hair;
Upon whose bosom snow has lain;
Who intimately lives with rain.

Poems are made by fools like me,
But only God can make a tree.

~Joyce Kilmer, 1886-1918~

Tower of Babel

When I was in high school, we were required to prepare a deck of vocabulary words. On the 3 by 5 cards we wrote a word on the front and the definition of the word on the back. We carried these cards with us to study new words and to make them a part of our vocabulary.

As adults our stacks of vocabulary cards kept growing as we got into jobs, married or moved into college and perhaps into graduate school.

My husband and I married as teen-agers, and raised seven children. I finally graduated from college after our children were grown, and I went to Seminary as a middle-aged widow.

Those of us who enrolled in Candler School of Theology (Emory University) remember our first class when Dr. William Mallard said, "When you go home today and you are asked what you learned in seminary you can say, 'uh Hermeneutics.'" So was added "hermeneutics" (without the "uh") and other theological words to our vocabulary. Mallard defined the word as "the science of the interpretation of Scripture or method of exegesis."

Let us imagine that each word in our vocabulary is on a 3 by 5 card and the cards are stacked in rows on a table. As we write and/or as we speak…even as I am writing…words are selected and combinations of words are used…to communicate…to convince…to tell a story…to relay a message.

All the words in our English language use only 26 letters. Everything we need to know - all the words used to express all meaning - can be said or written using only 26 letters. Yet it takes a thick dictionary to hold them all.

And we are sometimes speechless…inadequate when it comes to selecting the right word or combination of words and putting the words together to communicate effectively with one another.

I suppose all of us who have an interest in writing or speaking or in any communication, struggle with finding the right word…the correct combination of words…and with putting meaning into "words."

If we are a writer or a teacher, or a minister we might say, "Words are the tools of our trade." Churchill said, "Short words are best and old words are best of all." It was said of Churchill, "He mobilized the English language and sent it into battle."

Words! In these few minutes…as I have been writing, I have taken a stack …a pile of words…short words…old words…words that tend variety…and arranged them as prose. Prose is words which tend toward variety.

Poetry or verse in our culture is words arranged with repetition in their accent rhythm and which tend toward uniformity rather than variety.

The value of poetry is not confined to what is said. Equally as important is the language used …the words! Not just the meaning but being "surrounded by the words."

In the Old Testament book of Ruth, we might say "Ruth was homesick." But it is not the same as saying with Keats, "She stood in tears amid the alien corn."

We could say, "The sunrise was beautiful" but we catch our breath when Emily Dickinson wrote, "I'll tell you how the sun rose…A ribbon at a time."

I close this meditation with some words, some theology vocabulary words…arranged as verse. And I suppose it goes back to our society being inundated with words.

The first verse in the book of John tells us the prophets of old came generation after generation with words about God and many did not "get it." Then one day in the city of Bethlehem the Word was made flesh and we beheld his glory.

Could it be, "what we are sometimes building" is not a brave new world but a Tower of Babel?

Tower of Babel

I pile my poetry words… Up high
Theology words …Up to the sky.

And higher…High as eye can see
Hermeneutics, Exergesis, Theodicy!

Early on…Diversity…
The "cutting edge."…Plurality.

We add Process…Theology,
Post-Structuralist…Eschatology.

I clap my hands…My words have power,
I dance around…My poetry tower.

Confusion…Babel tumbles down.
My words lie silent…On the ground.

And kneeling there…in wordless loss,
I find the "WORD" …Beneath a cross!

~Ruth Baird Shaw~

Celebrations

Birthdays, Memorials and Family Events

Celebrating Christmas in Milstead, Georgia with Charles' family: From front left going clockwise around table: Lillian Shaw, Charles Shaw, me, Bill Shaw, James Shaw, Margaret Shaw, Grady Shaw, Jr., and Grady Shaw, Sr.

This last section of **The Chronicles of Ruth** *includes a birthday post for each of my seven children and other weblog pieces from* **Ruthlace** *to commemorate some family events.*

An 83rd Birthday Thanksgiving

One of the nice things about getting so old is that people start trying to find nice things to say about you on your birthday.

Like everyone else still breathing, I had a birthday this year. My birthday slipped up on me by stepping on the heels of last year's birthday. I tried to ignore it, but being blessed with many writers in our family, I had a well-documented and well-celebrated birthday! My Sunday birthday was celebrated the whole week-end.

My daughter, Carol (***The Median Sib***), got up early Sunday morning to click off 83 "random" things about me on her blog. She had to scrape the bottom on the barrel to find so many positive things to say.

Joan (***Daddy's Roses***) always knows what to say and how to say it. She wrote a flattering post about me, including pictures - one picture in a bathing suit (snapped by my husband more than a few years ago) and one more recent picture in a pulpit robe.

Other bloggers in the family, including my son Terrell (***Alone on a Limb***) and his wife, Sheila, and daughter, Lillian, were here to help celebrate.

Beth (***Blue Star Chronicles***) wrote "Happy Birthday Mother" and was here at our large gathering with her daughter, Amanda.

Actually I am delighted to be alive and enjoying life and I loved all the fanfare, gifts, books and flowers. The yellow tulip bouquet brought by Mike Bock from Ohio is a gift that keeps on giving as is the pot of pink kalanchoes from grandson Gil and his wife, Naomi, and sons, Lewis and Mark.

And the food! Carol prepared on Saturday night, the most fabulous dinner with her special chicken recipe with corn sticks, two great salads and a sour cream birthday cake with only 83 candles on it. She cooks with such ease and natural talent and invites everyone to share!

One of my sons-in-law (I have five) prepared the Sunday dinner of his tender beef roast, his special recipe for gravy, mashed potatoes etc. They (he and his wife, my daughter, Deborah) make their living writing, so they don't blog, but they always take time to help the family celebrate all the many occasions we find to celebrate.

My first daughter, Janice, and her husband, Gil, were here. Jan fits into the "professional writer" and "non-blogger" category too, although that is only a part of her professional profile. Jan was the most "beautiful and perfect" baby I had ever seen. She was born when I was still in my teens and her daddy was not quite 21. The tears of joy and amazement in her Daddy's eyes is a picture engraved on my heart. We were later to see six other "most beautiful and perfect" babies and a similar response from their Dad. When Jan and Gil would come to visit, her Dad would always introduce her as our "oldest daughter." Since "oldest' sounds negative and there is nothing negative about Jan, I decided to refer to her as "first daughter" on the rare occasions when I mention my children to a congregation of people.

An Ode to Daughters

I wrote "Ode to Daughters" for the annual UMW Mother-Daughter Banquet at Trinity Austell UMC at the request of the chair of programs.

An Ode to Our Daughters

An ode to our daughters
A "word bouquet"
How can I find
Words to convey ...

The worth of a daughter
The question asked
My mind could never
Meet the task.

My mind consulted
With my heart
And right away
Knew where to start.

Start at the beginning
When our baby girl
Was a dream in the heart
Of an unborn world!

"It's a girl," a wee baby
Just perfect . . . a girl!
I envisioned white ruffle
In a pink-ribboned world.

She's a girl . . . in pink softness
And colors . . . like these . . .
Red measles, yellow jaundice
And black and blue knees!

She's a girl . . . she is growing.
She is trying her wings,
Dear Lord, keep her safe
From life's hurts and stings.

She's a girl! She's a treasure . . .
That I recommend!
For she's always a daughter,
And more. She's a friend!

~Ruth Baird Shaw~

Happy Birthday To My Precious Son Terry on March 22!

Happy Birthday, Charles Terrell Shaw, on March 22nd. The picture on the left is one of his mother's favorites of him as a little boy.

We decided to call our first son, "Terry," although as an adult, he is Terrell. His sisters, Janice and Joan, were excited to have a baby brother and could not wait to hold him.

Terry was and still is everything any mother and father could wish for in a son…an adorable little boy, a good student, a boy scout, a loving brother to his six siblings and now an uncle to 16 nieces and nephews as well as great nephews and nieces.

He is also a good husband, father and church and community leader.

I am his mother, but I'm not alone in knowing Terrell Shaw as a notable citizen and outstanding teacher in our city's school system and also in singing and drama connected with our colleges' and city's fine arts programs.

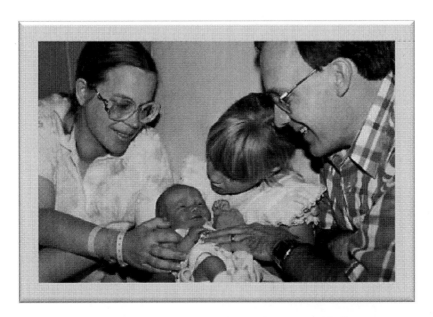

Terrell, his wife Sheila, and daughters, Brannon and Lillian

Did I mention Terrell has three beautiful and talented women (one wife and two daughters) in his life? He is also a dedicated school teacher, is often asked to sing at local events, and occasionally performs in local musicals and plays.

Happy Birthday to My Precious Son David on May 9!

David was born on a Friday afternoon at 3:00 p.m. - the seventh child and the second son of a Methodist pastor and his wife. This was at a time when pastors' salaries were very low even though ordination required 3 years of post-graduate seminary education.

But David was planned and welcomed as enthusiastically as if he were an only child. We brought him home from the hospital on Mother's Day over 40 years ago and I am still proud to be his mother.

David was a bright and happy boy who took seriously the fact that in the Bible "seven" is the number of perfection as well as completion.

As a boy, David preferred peanut butter sandwiches to vegetables and tried to live on them. This fact caused his Daddy to consult with a doctor friend. The doctor said he had heard of children who tried to survive on worse and David would grow out of it.

So he continued to push his veggies around on his

plate and drop as many as possible on the floor thinking his mother would not notice.

His sisters like to tease him at all family gatherings to this day that David never made his own peanut butter sandwiches. They report he enlisted one or another of his indulgent siblings to do it for him. As Carol said, "He was just so cute."

So David never needed "self-esteem" lessons or "diversity" training. He played the guitar and drum (and sometimes keyboard) in the RSV (Revised Standard Version) Youth Group musicals at church, and so was popular with his classmates and especially the girls as a teenager.

Today David is a hard working businessman, lay leader and active member of his church. He is

David and his wife Vicki have three daughters: Jessica, Katie and Haley

happily married to his lovely childhood sweetheart and the proud father of three beautiful daughters and now has a son-in-law and is the proud grandfather to James Alexander Rogers.

Opposites Attract

May 21, 2007

Today would have been my husband's 88th birthday. I thought I would honor Charles today by following the lead of my daughter, Joan, who wrote on her blog (***Daddy's Roses***) 13 differences in her and her spouse. In honor of Charles, here are some of our similarities and differences:

1. Movies. Charles loved movies, especially the old cowboy movies. I am not much of a movie fan. I have seen probably fewer than half a dozen in a theater in the last 20 years and not many more on television.

2. Seafood. Charles and I both liked sea food. We both grew up eating fish caught fresh from the Yellow River.

3. Sunday School. Like many pastors, he was not a regular in one Sunday School class. I enjoyed very much being a part of a Sunday School class from childhood on and have taught adult classes in all the churches where he was pastor.

4. Pets. Neither of us had much time for pets. We did have Hercules, a Chihuahua, when the children were small and later a German shepherd who followed David home from school. David named the big dog "Rex" (the name of his Dad's childhood dog) as soon as they arrived home. Rex loved to swim in the large lake in the neighborhood in East Point.

5. Vacation Spots. We both enjoyed camping and family gatherings. Charles also loved fishing and hunting and once caught an 18 inch Brown Trout in an Ellijay mountain stream, much to the delight of our children and some of the neighbor children who were splashing in the water. He had the fish mounted by Rev. Bob Cagle, who had answered the call to preach as a student and, from childhood, was a member of our UMC in Ellijay.

6. Temperature. I am the cold-natured one who now wears long sleeves even in the summer. This may be an old age thing.

7. Time of Day. He was a night owl; I am an early bird. When he was in seminary at Candler, he would stay up all night writing papers or studying for an exam. On the other hand, I went to Seminary after his death and would go to bed early and get up at 4 to write any paper that required creativity.

8. Food. We both thoroughly enjoyed a dinner of fresh turnip greens and cornbread with a glass of buttermilk as a complete meal after our children were all out of the nest. A meal with dried beans cooked from scratch as the main course was also a welcomed meal to both of us. We failed in passing along the love of fresh greens and that wonderful bean source of protein to our children.

9. Family of Origin. I am the youngest of nine and the only one still living. Charles was the oldest of five boys – all of them now gone. My father died when I was 9, but Charles and I both had strong family ties with parents and siblings.

10. TV Shows. He enjoyed the old cowboy and war movies or shows like **Gunsmoke** and **M.A.S.H.** I prefer a situation comedy like **Designing Women** or **Matlock** with Andy Griffith.

11. Health. He had serious hearing and ear problems from World War II experiences. His first heart attack and by-pass surgery was at age 59 and his final one at age 67. Most of my health issues (except for painful trigeminal neuralgia episodes from 1990 on) have been after age 82.

12. Religion. Both of us were/are very serious, some might say "overly serious," Christians.

13. Blog. I enjoy all forms of writing and still write! I doubt that he would have gotten into blogging as he left much of the family writing (Christmas letters, thank you notes, etc.) up to me. He was an outgoing and charismatic extrovert. I am more introverted. He would sometimes have me edit pastoral reports and letters while he made sick calls. However he read widely - books of theology and the Bible and could quote much of it and was gifted in Biblical preaching.

A Tribute to Charles Columbus Shaw

(May 21, 1919 – December 3, 1986)

Here are some little known facts about Charles Shaw in reply to a letter from one of his children.

His basic Marine Corps training was in San Diego.

Charles had a lot of leadership skills. When he was inducted at Fort Mac, they gave him the choice of what branch of service he wanted to serve in. He chose the Marines. He was put in charge of a group that was traveling together to the Marine base in San Diego, California.

His later service was in the South Pacific until the end of the war in 1945. He told us the medals pictured on one of his uniforms to the left were not for meritorious service but were given to all who survived the rigors of boot camp.

Charles Shaw served two years in the Marine Corps from 1943-1945. I think his leadership qualities must have been recognized because he only had a high school education at the time.

When he was in the Marine Corps, he wrote a letter to me nearly every day. The 15 months he was overseas he wrote as often as possible - sometimes several times a week. We were both letter writers. I wrote to him every day. I am sorry we did not keep the letters.

When Charles was a teenager, he would often write the "love letters" for many of his buddies. Writing letters was a common way of communicating then. He wrote me a letter every week while we were dating.

I wish I had kept the letter he wrote telling me how much he liked the biscuits I had made that my friend Julia insisted he must eat. I had apologized for Julia making him eat one of my biscuits. As soon as he got home that Sunday evening he wrote how much he liked the biscuit, and then he added, "I would eat anything to be near you."

Another thing Charles Shaw did as a teenager which shows his uniqueness was to "adopt" a child at the Methodist Children's Home. There must have been something presented in church about the need. Anyway, he asked to "adopt a child" and used some of his hard earned money to buy toys and clothes for the child they assigned him. I suspect many of those who chose to participate in the "adopt a child" project of the church were people older and with more money.

Charles in front of the Ellijay parsonage with Carol, David, Debi and Terry

He was a wonderfully tender hearted man. And he was a worker! He delivered newspapers as a young boy. Later he had a dry cleaning route where he went around from house to house and collected clothes his customers wanted cleaned and took them to a dry cleaner company in Conyers. Later in the week he went back to Conyers to get the cleaned clothes. He delivered them and collected the payments. He made only a pittance but every little bit helped.

As soon as he was old enough, he went to work for Calloway Mills. He made the amazing salary of 25 cents an hour. As was common in those depression years, he gave all his paychecks to his dad and mother to help with household expenses. They then gave him back some "spending money." He did this right up to the week we were married.

I have wondered WHY we did not save his Marine stuff for posterity. It was not a time when one thought about family history as much as we do now. Mainly we did not think of family history because there was not as much leisure time then as now. In other words, we were busy making history.

We led such a full life with his taking advantage of the Veterans' Bill of Rights to go back to school and finish college and then going for 3 years more of seminary and such busy pastorates which he continued after two heart attacks and bypass surgery and until his death on December 3, 1986.

Happy Valentine Day

When I was asked to write a poem for our 1976 Valentine Banquet program for pastors and spouses, I came up with a poem that is a favorite of my children and many friends. The poem is, by design, a fun piece about married love and is full of clichés and inside jokes for pastors. I hope it adds to the charm of the poem.

WE

I was I and he was he . . . A ceremony made us "we."
When in the sight of God and men . . .
We pledged our troth and kissed our kin
And set our sails . . . breathlessly
On the matrimony sea.

My handsome prince . . . He held my hand.
My every wish . . . was his command
Until one day . . . I said, "I think we . . .
Should see my friends . . . More frequently.

He said, so loud . . . It shook the house
That he was man . . . and not a mouse
And furthermore . . . he said we should
See his friends more . . . he said we would.

He said, we would . . . most certainly
I said, we won't . . . We both said "we"
Strange, when we do . . . Or don't agree
One thing is clear . . . We both say "we"

Now that's the secret . . . For love to grow
Through Summer's sun . . . and Winter's snow
Through diaper rash . . . And teething ills
From P.T.A. . . . to college bills

Through three-point circuits . . . And inner-city
And Pastor Parish Relations Committee
Through Conference moving time . . . again
When you're not one . . . of the bishop's men.

Through covered dishes . . . Well, thick and thin
Love like this . . . will never end
For when we do . . . or don't agree . . .
We still find joy . . . in being '"we".

~by Ruth Baird Shaw~

Tribute to my Nephew, Don Baird

William Donald Baird: February 10, 1936 - March 28, 2008

When I was not quite 13, I was excited to welcome into our family a wonderful little boy who was born to my 31-year old brother, William Bogan Baird (called Willie B), and his wife, Wylene McCart Baird. Bill was called Willie B. until he got tired of it late in life and was known as Bill.

Don was their only child. Below is some of the information from my son Terrell's blog, **Alone on a Limb.** Terrell describes Don as "soft spoken" but he also had a great speaking and singing voice.

Don grew up to be one of the finest news reporters WSB had in the historic era of the 1960s. He is best remembered for his coverage of Lester Maddox - which launched him into national fame on the NBC Radio Network where he was a constant free-lance contributor.

Don himself recalls some highlights: "Taping a sprinting Lester Maddox as he chased black people from his restaurant... describing a mob scene as whites beat blacks at a "patriotic rally" at Lakewood Park ... holding MLK's peace prize during an interview. . . covering his funeral on loan to NBC.

Don had worked for the Atlanta Journal Constitution for several years before he joined WSB. From WSB he went on to work for the network reporting for NBC from their Cleveland, Ohio bureau. The last decade or more of his career was spent with CNN Radio.

Don was a true gentleman. He was soft-spoken, thoughtful, and kind. He was endlessly entertaining and interesting with his stories of covering famous people and events, and his interest in the unusual in Georgia history. Besides writing news he also wrote songs and poems and had several book ideas he was kicking around. I hope that some of his unfinished writing will make its way into print, or, at least, cyber print, so that some of his unique knowledge will be preserved.

We will all miss this truly good man.

Tribute to Ray Warren Lathem III

October 19, 1975 – May 11, 1996

All of us who know and love Jane and Warren and who knew their parents were in shock and grief with them on May 11th of 1996 when we got the word that the oldest of their two sons, Ray Warren Lathem III, and other missionaries were on the ValuJet plane that crashed in the Florida Everglades.

On October 19, 1975 at 3:33 a.m., Ray W. Lathem III was born to Warren and Jane Baird Lathem. Jane wrote about that happy day:

> *I gave birth to my first child. I was young and scared to death but also thrilled and very happy. We only celebrated 20 birthdays with him but we are thankful for each one. Happy Birthday Ray! We love you, miss you and look forward to seeing you again.*

Warren Lathem wrote on May 11, 2011:

> *Fifteen years ago today life changed forever for the Lathems when Ray, Carlos Gonzales, Roger and Dana Lane died along with 106 more people in the ValuJet crash in the Florida Everglades. Today there is a service of remembrance in the Everglades at the Memorial, a beautiful concrete structure designed by students at the U of M School of Architecture. One of their classmates died in the crash. We were there for the 10th anniversary. We will not be there for this one. Jane and I leave Monday for work at the Seminario de Wesleyano de Venezuela where we have been building a living memorial for the past several years. God has done an amazing work of grace in our lives through this tragedy. We still grieve, but not as those who have no hope. Our hope is secure. Ray, we love you and miss you, but we will see you again in a little while. In the meantime, there is Kingdom work to do and we are committed to doing it as long as we have breath.*

The over flowing Mt Pisgah church sanctuary for Ray's Home Going Service in May 1996 was only a small token of the love and sorrow so many were feeling and continue to feel in the death of such a precious and talented young man. At the time of Ray's death, he was returning from a Christian Mission trip to Venezuela. Ray was a gifted student, singer and poet.

I was in Cedartown with the Lathems for the celebration of my brother Tom Baird's 80ths birthday and heard Ray's wonderful Christian testimony about his missionary call just a couple of weeks before the ValuJet crash.

Ray Lathem III

To me it did not seem "right" that my big brother Tom's family has had to deal with a sudden family death again. I well remember being the one who had to tell my mother about Tom and Rowena's son and Jane's brother, Jack's accident and death at age 22 in 1964.

My mother, a devout Christian was "angry with God" when I told her about Jack. Why our precious Jack? Jack was such an adorable little boy and Mama doted on him and loved to recount all his brilliant and cute sayings. Tom Baird's wife, Rowena, had lived with his mother while Rowena was pregnant and gave birth to Jack while Tom was serving in Europe in World War II. Mama loved Rowena like her own daughter.

While riding from the crowded Methodist church to the cemetery after Jack's Service in Cedartown, Georgia, with a dozen or more Georgia State Patrol cars leading the way, my mind was in turmoil as I kept praying for my dear brother, sister-in-law , their little daughter, Jane, the grandmothers and all the shocked and grieving family.

Praying also for answers to the "whys" of a young person's death? Among many other passages of Scripture, Psalm 90 spoke to me then and spoke to me later as I sat in the sanctuary just a few rows behind Tom and Rowena, Warren, Jane and Jared in another overflow crowd at Mt Pisgah Church in Alpharetta, Georgia at the Home Going Service for our precious Ray Lathem in 1996.

Moses wrote in Psalm 90, "A thousand years in God's sight are but as a day when it is past and as a watch in the night." God has made us for eternity and our swift run across the stage of earth - whether just a few months in our mother's womb (as two babies I have conducted burial services for) or a 98 year old man we buried from Trinity church recently - is as a day in the sight of God. In the case of Ray, it is merely the first notes on a beautiful symphony yet to be played.

It seems to me that measuring the length of life in the light of eternity - whether we live a hundred years or just twenty or thirty years - we have only a brief time. This is why it is so important to learn from God. The eternal God is our dwelling place and underneath is the everlasting arms.

God has given us freedom. We are in a highly mechanized, fallen world and it seems to me many persons' physical lives are cut short needlessly. Human error is said to have been the cause of the airplane crash that took the physical life of Ray and other missionaries to Venezuela. Questions!

Praise God what we call "Death" does not have the final word about what God calls "Life." Jesus took away the sting of death when He said in John 11:25: "I am the resurrection and the life, those who believe in Me, though they die, yet shall they live."

A Mother's Day Glimpse of My Mother

Happy Mother's Day! Each of us is either the son or the daughter of a mother; so in that capacity all of us fit into a Mother's Day celebration. As a mother myself, I have had a difficult time with some of the sermons I have heard on Mother's Day. They make all mothers sound like "angels." One would get the idea that to become a mother is to become a saint.

Erma Bombeck said, "The easiest part of being a mother is giving birth. The hardest part is showing up on the job every day." And I might add it is showing up 24/7. We all know there are loving, hardworking, good mothers and there are also selfish and neglectful and even abusive mothers. Most of us, as mothers, find our place somewhere in between.

At the same time, there is something about motherhood that tends to bring out the best in us. The seemingly endless nausea, misery and pain of pregnancy and childbirth mixed with that incredible love that we have for that helpless and amazingly beautiful baby when it is finally born is awesome. It is awesome to be a mother. No wonder so many of us feel so inadequate we fall on our knees and seek the wisdom of God.

Many of us - probably most of us as adults - have an emotional attachment and love for our mother. And in cases where the mother has such personal problems as to neglect, abuse or abandon the child, there is always unbelievable sorrow. In cases where the mother dies while the child is young, there is a great feeling of loss. Just the thought of "mother" brings about great emotion in many of us.

I remember one morning a few days before Mother's Day when I was sitting in the sanctuary at Grantville with our church music director. We were discussing the music for Mother's Day and got into a conversation about some of the old time songs about mothers. She mentioned two of the old gospel songs from her childhood: "That Silver-Haired Mother of Mine" and "If I Could Hear My Mother Pray Again." We both choked up with tears in our eyes. Mother sees possibilities in us that other people seem not to notice. In much the same way, God sees possibilities in us that we do not see in ourselves and others fail to see.

Happy Mother's Day 2009

God bless the memory of my dear mother, Ieula Ann Dick Baird (March 6, 1885 - December 7, 1973).

I never knew Mama as the young woman in the photo on the right. She was 37 when I was born as the 11th child born to her and my father, Benjamin Wilson Baird.

Ieula Ann Dick Baird

My mother gave me a Bible story book to read to my children when our oldest was just a toddler. The book had the little poem below about the importance of reading to children. I tried to follow this advice but as time went on, regretfully, I did not find time to read to our children as often as I would have liked to do.

You may have tangible wealth untold,
Caskets of jewels and coffers of gold.
Richer than I, you can never be,
I had a mother who read to me.

~ Strickland Gillilan (1869-1954) ~

My mother did not read a great deal to me, even though, in a community where not many books were available, there were always books in our home in addition to the worn Bible. Mama, holding down a full time job, was a reader and would read something out loud to us from the daily newspaper or a Christian

Ruth Baird Shaw

publication. She also told me stories. I have related on **Ruthlace** (my weblog) most of the family stories she told me. After my father died, she told me stories about her life as a little girl as we slept in the same double bed in our smaller home.

My mother had also been raised by a widowed mother. Her young father had died when she was only 18 months old and while her mother was pregnant with her youngest brother. There were also four older sisters and an older brother. She was reared in a small house on her maternal grandfather's large farm.

Mama once told how, as a little girl, she would sometimes rub her mother's cold feet to warm them on freezing winter nights. She adored her hard working mother.

With tears in her eyes, Mama also told me of the last time she saw her mother. She had watched her mother's horse and buggy out of sight down the long dusty road in front of their modest country home. When

My mother, Ieula Baird, standing in her yard in Porterdale, Georgia

she got word her mother was dying (around 1917), Mama took a train from their home in Oak Hill (near Conyers), but her mother had already died when she arrived in Griffin.

My daughter, Deborah Lewis, wrote a book in 1990 titled **Motherhood Stress**. It was later put out in paperback which I think is one of the best on the subject. On the cover is a woman stretched out across two mountain peaks, with children walking across her, and the subtitle is *Finding Encouragement in the Ultimate Helping Profession.* Motherhood is the ultimate helping profession, and parents are encouraged to realize the importance of the job.

I was in my early fifties when my mother died at age 88. Even though I had a husband and seven children, I will never forget the sense of loneliness and loss I felt to realize my mother was no longer in my world.

My mother had a philosophy of life as a Christian, not to worry about things that "could not be helped" and to take each day as a new beginning. In her honor, I want to include a ballad I wrote in 1983 to honor my mother.

A Ballad for my Mother

1. My mother grew old. . . had lines etched in her face
Worked hard all her life. . . with uncommon grace
She lived by the Bible. . . Each day and each mile
She taught me her secret. . . of life with a smile

Refrain:

Today is the first day. . . Of the rest of your life
Don't borrow trouble. . . With yesterday's strife
Take time, smell the flowers. . . It makes life worth while
Pick up each new day. . . With love and a smile

2. Widowed while young. . . Mama worked in a mill
Washed on a scrub-board. . . Brought wood up a hill
She sang as she labored. . . to stay out of debt
She taught me a lesson. . . I'll never forget.

Refrain:

3. One day I said, "Mama,. . . Your life has been hard.
You've buried two babies. . . Out in the church yard.

You've known all the heartache. . . of struggling for bread."
She smiled through her tears and these words she said:

Refrain

4. Her old fashioned teacakes? We ate the last crumb!
Her old fashioned flowers? She had a green thumb!
She lived by the Bible. . . Each day and each mile.
She taught me her secret. . . of life with a smile.

Refrain

~Ruth Baird Shaw~

Happy Birthday to My Precious Daughter Janice on June 3!

Janice was our first baby. She was born to Charles and me just ten months after our wedding. I was young, and Charles was only 4 years older. We had much to learn, but we both were idealistic and eager to learn to be good parents. Janice, a bright, beautiful and outgoing child, learned to walk and talk early.

With no children to play with at home, Janice slipped out of the yard to visit and talk to all the neighbors - children as well as the adults. With her shy mother close behind her, she taught me how to make friends with all my neighbors.

Janice as a child

Janice in her 20s

My wise mother mentioned to me one day that she had tried to teach her children many things but found she had also learned much from each of them.

I can say the same because, early on, Janice taught her young shy mother how to be neighborly. In fact, today, when people compliment me for being "smart" because I went back to school and earned college and seminary degrees after my children were

Janice, her husband, Gilbert, and their seven grandchildren

grown, I tell them I have been taught so much by my wonderful children, starting with the first, Janice, and straight through to the youngest, David.

Janice was, and still is, a daughter to make her parents proud. She was, and still is, a loving "big sister" to her younger siblings, setting an example of excellence in school and in life.

Happy Birthday to our precious daughter Janice - now wife, mother and grandmother as well as a Christian leader and gifted speaker.

A Father's Legacy

Happy Father's Day! We all come to Father's Day thinking about our own dad or the man or men in our lives who gave us love and protection as a child, rather than thinking about some honor due us if we also happen to be a father.

David Blankenhorn wrote a book titled ***Fatherless America.*** He states that when a father dies (unlike when a father voluntarily is absent or leaves), his fatherhood lives on in the head and the heart of his child as family and friends seek to keep his memory alive and find ways to help compensate for the father's absence. He says that in this sense the child is still fathered.

I recently read an article titled "A Father's Death Leaves Love Behind." William Maddox wrote about his father-in-law, a man he never met because the dad died when his daughter was only three. The man had been a musician who sang in a quartet and had cut a few records. William Maddox said that his wife's father's legacy lived on because his words and deeds and music had a profound influence on his wife's upbringing. The father died young, but he left a legacy of love behind.

My father, Benjamin Wilson Baird, had a profound influence on me even though he died when I was nine. I would hear other children say, "I want to be a nurse" or "I want to be a policeman when I grow up," and I would think, "I want to be a Christian like Papa." His Christian influence was a greater legacy for me than any amount of money or property he could have left me.

My father did not want to leave his wife and children, but as heart disease weakened his body, he was so certain of heaven that he looked forward to death as one would anticipate a long-awaited vacation. He knew that what we call "death" does not have the last word over what God calls "Life."

My father, Benjamin Wilson Baird

Looking back I know I was profoundly influenced and still fathered in some sense by my mother telling me about my father. In normal conversation, Mama would often mention to me events in his day-to-day life to illustrate how dearly he loved her and how he loved and prayed for me and for all their children. She told me he was a hard-working and gifted farmer always working to provide for his family during those depression years.

My mother's dad also died when she was a baby. Mama told me that when other children would wear a new dress or shoes and say, "My daddy bought these for me," she would feel sad and think, "If my papa was still alive, I would have new things too."

At a memorial service at our church conference a few years ago, Bishop Bevel Jones preached, and one of the things he said was about Aristotle Onassis, who, amid his millions, never had a cause he supported. Jones said, "To leave no estate is not a disgrace, but to leave no legacy is a tragedy."

I am glad for movements like Promise Keepers and other movements among men to help them and to help us all realize how much men are needed in the lives of children; to help us all realize how rewarding it is for men to grow old with offspring who love and respect them because of the love and attention they gave when their children were young.

I vividly remember one father who, with his wife, was a member of a church where I was pastor for four years. They had two daughters. Both were beautiful young married women with 2 children each. Several times a year, and especially every Father's Day, these two daughters and their entire family drove a great distance to proudly sit with their dad on Father's Day. These daughters' loving attention to their dad in his old age spoke volumes to me about a father's legacy.

Ruth Baird Shaw

Happy Birthday to My Precious Daughter Carol on Aug. 26!

Carol is our middle child with a brother and two sisters older than she and two sisters and a brother younger. Carol has titled her popular weblog **The Median Sib,** but there is nothing middle about her except being the fourth of seven children born to her daddy and me. On a scale of one to ten, she is an eleven! Never a four!

I'm holding Carol in this photo from 1952

Carol was a beautiful baby and a very feminine little girl with blond curly hair. She was as wonderfully precocious as her own son and daughter and the three precious little granddaughters she now loves to be with and to write about on Facebook.

Carol is more like me in size (four other daughters being shorter in height as was their paternal grandmother and other women in the family). Carol is about five feet six as am I. Carol also shares my love for cooking. She is a fabulous and innovative cook.

Also, as Joan of **Daddy's Roses** fame pointed out, Carol - and Joan, too - share my reserved nature; so they may actually "understand me" somewhat better than their 5 more gregarious siblings.

However, as we all know, none of us are limited by being "reserved" or "gregarious" but all of us are a combination of both with unlimited possibilities though the grace of Christ.

All those who have grown children know that they all think (whether they are reserved or gregarious) that they understand their parents only too well.

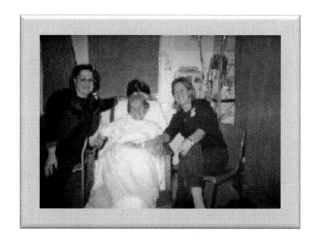

But I am blessed beyond measure to love and have a good relationship with all seven of my children and my five sons-in-law and two daughters -in - law.

In 2001, Carol took time off to drive me to Johns Hopkins Hospital in Baltimore from my home in Georgia for Trigeminal surgery by Dr. Ben Carson. Carol and I spent a few days of recuperation with daughter Janice and her family in Maryland.

Happy Birthday, Carol! Carol is a beautiful woman, an outstanding teacher and talented writer and has a great "Erma Bombeck" sense of humor illustrated in many of her articles published in the Nashville paper a few years ago. She is also the talented editor of my last two books, **Life with Wings** and **The Chronicles of Ruth.**

Carol and her husband Ron have three granddaughters: Lily, Sophie and Evey

Wedding in New Hampshire

Eleven of our eighteen grandchildren are now married. (2011) I have not been able to attend several of the weddings because of the distance involved. One of the weddings (Joey and Meleah Johnston) was in Hawaii. One wedding (Josh and Michaela Hearn) was in Germany and another (Amanda and Brian Sims) in Nevada. More recently, I was unable to attend the June 2011 wedding on our grandson, Jonathan Lewis, to Jessica Young in High Bridge, Kentucky.

I was able to attend the "Wedding in Alabama" of our beautiful granddaughter, Jessica Shaw, to Philip Rogers at their United Methodist Church near Jacksonville State College on May 19, 2007 - only an hour and a half from my home. The wedding was beautiful with a fabulous wedding reception in Anniston, Alabama.

Jessica and Philip

After a couple of years of health issues, I had not planned to make the long journey north to attend the wedding of our grandson Matthew Lewis to Emily Brown on 7/7/07.

However, thanks to the insistence and assistance of Janice and Gilbert and Deborah and Gregg, I did attend and had a great time traveling to New Hampshire and Vermont for their wedding in the historic chapel at Dartmouth College.

I rode with Deborah and Gregg up to Maryland on July 3rd and stayed with Janice and Gilbert while the Lewises went on to New Hampshire to get ready for the rehearsal dinner.

Gil and Jan and I had dinner on the Fourth of July with Charmaine and Jack (granddaughter) and family and saw the City of Arlington, Virginia fireworks. I was pleased to see them and five of my great grandchildren in their new home and again when they came over on Sunday to eat and swim at Jan and Gil's.

Gilbert, Janice and I left on Friday morning, July 6, to get to Dartmouth in time for the rehearsal and rehearsal dinner. This country girl had never visited New York City. So Gil, my gallant son-in-law, decided to leave early enough to show me the highlights of the Big Apple. We drove through Central Park, past the huge United Nations Buildings, the Theater district - well everything I had read about but never seen, including the Statue of Liberty in the harbor.

Gregg and Debi hosted a rehearsal dinner at a restaurant near Dartmouth. In keeping with Emily and Matthew's request, it was a casual but delicious sit down dinner of pizza, pasta, and salads for nearly 50. Deborah had requested and received 70 plus pictures of Emily from Mrs. Brown so she and Jonathan created a masterpiece 12-minute video featuring Emily and Matthew from birth to now. It was quite a feat of creativity with music. We enjoyed a tour of the beautiful Dartmouth campus between the rehearsal and the dinner.

Jan and Gil and I stayed with Mike and Brenda Cline, church friends of Matthew and Emily. They live in what they described to us as a "Yankee barn" type of house - lots of windows, surrounded by trees. It was a joy to visit with them. It was "Southern hospitality" at its best in New Hampshire!

After sleeping on beds of the "Rich and Famous" for a full week, I am like the little girl from Milstead who went to Atlanta to visit her married brother and sister-in-law for a week. When she got home and sat again at the family table, she commented, "I have dined out so much it is hard to eat Mama's cooking."

Gilbert and Janice also have a pillow-top mattress on the queen size bed in their guest room where I resided in luxury. I slept like a baby every night! Well not exactly. You know how a baby sleeps? Sleeps an hour and cries an hour! I slept two more nights in the luxurious home and on the same kind of pillow-top mattress in the home of these new friends in New Hampshire! So I slept well every night away from home.

You all know how I hesitate to be a participant in our "decadent consumer society" (a seminary term,) but I am thinking (like the little Milstead girl) that after seven nights on pillow top mattresses, my 25-year-old mattress may have to be replaced. Perhaps I will go out tomorrow and spend my children's inheritance on a new mattress!

Matthew and Emily

The wedding on Saturday night was beautiful. Did I mention they had the best soloist in America? Ask anyone in Rome! Terrell Shaw sang, *Great is thy Faithfulness* and *The Lord's Prayer*. We arrived early on a very warm day (thinking the wedding was 4 instead of 4:30,) so Gil (remarkable man that he is) opened both side doors and turned on the fans so that the chapel had cooled off before people started arriving.

Emily was very lovely! Stunning! Her dress was gorgeous with short cap sleeves, rounded neck, long train, and a delicate embroidery design.

Emily's bridesmaids' dresses were a simple design in light green – the same shade as our Granddaughter Jessica had her bridesmaids wear at her beautiful wedding two months earlier to Philip Rogers.

Matthew looked handsome in a gray tux; the groomsmen looked great in gray suits. Benjamin and Jonathan were ushers and also looked nice in gray suits with green shirts.

Emily's grandfather and our dear Lisette each read a short passage of scripture. The ceremony was similar to our beautiful Methodist ceremony. Their pastor also gave a meaningful short sermon and celebrated Holy Communion with them while Terrell sang *The Lord's Prayer.*

It rained off and on all day -- but never when we had to be outside. The reception was at a museum nearby and was very nice with a large group of over 100 present. A buffet of barbecue and chicken and a vegetable shish-kabob with salads was served. We had wonderful fellowship and food. People could enjoy the museum or go into the community room for the reception and dinner.

We caravanned back to Jan and Gil's on Sunday morning with the Lewises through Pennsylvania and more wonderful scenery. We enjoyed talking, listening to music and recounting all the great aspects of the Dartmouth wedding of Matthew and Emily.

Gladys and Lavay's 50th Wedding Anniversary

A few Comments of Memory and Appreciation

Congratulations to Gladys and Lavay on their 50th wedding anniversary! Lavay is my nephew and the oldest of my parents' twenty grandchildren, so he had his own special place in the Baird family.

Gladys and Lavay on their wedding day

After Lavay and Gladys's marriage, Gladys also became a vital and beautiful part of our large family. I am especially appreciative of the fact that Lavay and Gladys visited (and later brought their children to visit) his widowed maternal grandmother regularly in her old age.

Gladys and Lavay and their children - Belinda, Laura and Andy - also could always be counted on to participate and attend Baird family reunions, funerals and weddings when possible.

Lavay is the only child of my sister Louise and her husband, Ernest McCullough. Louise was the last of my three sisters and five brothers to die. So, as his last aunt who knew him as a child, I will write a few memories of Lavay's childhood.

Lavay came into the world with a ready-made and large family of fans. His mother Louise, as the oldest daughter, was called "Sis" by the rest of us. Sis, the perfect lady, took an interest in her younger siblings and tried to teach us proper manners, not always with success. Nevertheless, she had a special place in the heart of each one of us. I will miss her as long as I live!

Lavay's dad was killed in a tragic robbery when Lavay was a baby. Lavay may know more of the details from his mother than I, but my understanding is that Ernest was robbed of his money by two brothers and killed. The two Hulsey brothers received the death penalty and were electrocuted for this horrible crime.

One of the sad memories of my childhood is the sight of my grieving sister, Louise, fainting and almost falling as she was being escorted to a car supported on each side by her two older brothers (Wilson Grice and William Bogan) to go to the first of the cars lined up in front of our house on 32 Hazel Street to go to the funeral of her husband's and the father of her baby.

When Lavay was less than two, he contracted polio in an epidemic among babies and young children. The "new" disease was affecting many babies at that time and was introduced to us as "Infantile Paralysis."

The treatment then was to isolate the child with polio because of fear of contagion. I remember my mother being furious with the medical people at the hospital because they took him screaming away from his mother and would not let her stay with him. The family story is he never stopped crying and his strong voice could be heard crying loudly enough to be heard all the way to the waiting room.

Apparently it helped to develop his lungs to prepare him for his later calling as a preacher of the Gospel. So I suppose Mama finally forgave them. After they brought Lavay home, Sis made up for any trauma he may have endured as she lovingly bathed and massaged his legs every night.

Sis was reluctant, but Mama loved, to tell stories of the "cute" things Lavay said as a handsome and bright little boy who learned to talk early. Mama told about how Lavay, as a toddler, slipped out of his mother's reach as she was giving him a bath, ran "stark naked" out the door to the back porch and yelled to Mrs. Horning,

This photo is of me at age 8 next to Lavay, age 2

a neighbor, "Look Horning, I'm barefooted."

Louise and Mama took joy in the fact that Lavay, in spite of his paralyzed leg, learned to do exceptionally well everything any other boy could do, including bicycling and climbing trees.

Lavay's grandfather (my father), Wilson Baird, became ill with heart disease and died in 1932 when Lavay was only three. Family members told me how, as a thoughtful man who loved all children, Papa gave special love and attention and prayer for Lavay as his first grandchild as well as to the other three grandchildren (Marian Loyd, Leon Loyd and Bobby Baird) who were toddlers and the only grandchildren born before my father died. Papa was bedridden over a year before he died.

My sister Vera told me how several of the little children were one day beside Papa's bed playing when she went into his room. She said, "Papa, I'm so sorry. Are they bothering you?" He replied, "Let them stay with me. We are having an important conversation."

Veteran's Day 2005

In Honor of My Marine on Veteran's Day

There are really no words to describe my feelings and probably the feelings of many widows of World War II veterans as we contemplate Veteran's Day 2005. They tell me that over 1000 World War II veterans are dying daily now. Those living are in their eighties. However, to me they are still young men like my grandson, Josh, who is serving in the Army in Germany. They are still those idealistic, brave, vital young soldiers who willingly went off to war believing that they were helping to assure the safety and freedom of their families. They were willing to serve in spite of great personal sacrifice. They were certainly a part of one of the greatest generations in our country's history.

Four of my school friends were killed in World War II – James Homer Cook, Quinton "Red" Cole, Carroll Adams and J.W. Rye. My brother, Tom, served in the infantry. He and his wife, Rowena, married just before he went into the Army. Rowena lived with my mother, her new mother-in-law, while Tom was away. My brother, Jack, served in the Army Air force. These are just some of the men we also honor this Veteran's Day.

When President Roosevelt came on the radio early Sunday morning on December 7, 1941 and announced that the Japanese had bombed Pearl Harbor, life in the towns and cities of America was forever changed. I vividly remember the terror and anxiety I felt. We'd never before been in war in my lifetime. No one knew what might be next, and so days were filled with fear and uncertainty. We were afraid that our mainland would be bombed next.

In the days, weeks, and months that followed, the entire population rallied around the President and our national leadership. Patriotism was strong. Citizens supported whatever the President felt should be done. The immediate response of our nation to the bombing of Pearl Harbor was somewhat like the national response to the events of September 11, 2001, when everyone pulled together and supported one another. We were all uncertain what would happen next and wondered how our individual lives were going to be changed. Winning the war seemed to be the only focus of the entire population.

Soon the military draft was begun. Women were never drafted, but many volunteered to serve in the WACS and WAVES. Able-bodied young men were eager to sign up. It was the right and patriotic thing to do. They felt a desire, a need and an obligation to protect their families and their country from threat and to ensure our way of life. Charles was in line early the morning they opened the draft. Because of this he got a low draft number. However, as his number came up and before he could be drafted, he, like many others, opted to volunteer instead so that he could choose his branch of service.

In 1943 Charles and three of his buddies from our hometown, Grover Foster, Charlie Miller and Roy Connell, were sent to Cherry Point, NC. Later they were stationed in San Diego. Charlie Miller was wounded in the battle of Iwo Jima and was never well again. These four young fathers joined countless others giving years of their lives for the good of their country.

Charles with a Marine buddy in the South Pacific

When we learned that Charles was to be shipped to the South Pacific without a furlough, I went out to be with him in San Diego. On the way there (a four day train ride), I came down with scarlet fever. As soon as I arrived at the Marine base, I was quarantined for 21 days. Charles' first assignment in the South Pacific was in the Caroline Islands.

Back at home, food and gasoline were in short supply because the nation's resources were going toward the war effort. The government issued ration books to citizens who then had to use the coupons to get supplies such as sugar and gasoline.

Some textile mills switched over to making strong canvas for tents instead of fabrics for civilian clothing, and some mills made cord which was used to reinforce tires for military vehicles. Almost all the factories switched from making goods for regular civilian use to making needed military supplies.

The focus of daily life was to keep abreast of what was happening overseas. I remember reading the newspapers from cover to cover every day to find out what was happening and discussing the events with other adults with whom I came into contact in the course of the day. All ears were tuned to the radio anytime a report or a speech came on. There were great, inspiring, and encouraging speeches by Roosevelt and Churchill.

Every night I sat down and wrote a letter to my Marine. Every morning I dressed my two little girls and walked to the post office to mail that letter and see if we had a letter from "Daddy."

Citizens spent whatever free time they had doing whatever they could to help with the war effort. Some worked for the Red Cross. Patriotic and Christian groups frequently had rallies and services to support the troops and to encourage each other.

Children's lives were very different with few male influences, and the constant talk of war made many of them fearful. A whole generation of children lived without the benefit of their fathers. And those fathers gave up precious early years of their children's lives in order to preserve freedom for our country.

My daughter, Joan, who was not quite 2 years old when her daddy left, didn't understand what "war" was all about, of course. So when my brother, Jack, came home on furlough, she kept looking behind him, asking, "Where's Daddy?" Apparently she expected all the soldiers to come marching home in a line.

Finally the war was over. There were community and church celebrations throughout the country. I clearly remember the celebration service our community held. The entire community gathered at the Baptist church in Milstead to thank the Lord for the end of the war. Charles was home on furlough at the time, and our complete family attended together. It was quite a celebration!

Charles had to return to Cherry Point and be mustered out before he could come home for good.

Charles often said in the years after the war that "buddies" in the service are more than "buddies" – they are brothers. They all seemed to feel a strong sense of brotherhood and connection with each other, realizing that their very lives were in each other's hands.

This is what Veteran's Day 2005 means to me. It means recognition of the sacrifices made – by the soldiers, their families, their children, and the nation as a whole. It means appreciation for what thousands of our fellow citizens have done and are doing for me – for US – for their country – not just in World War II but in other wars our country has fought and is fighting to preserve our freedoms and the freedoms of people throughout the world. I pray that they shall not have lived and fought in vain.

In Memory of My Dear Sister

I am the last of eleven siblings in my family. Two died in infancy. Rowena was the wife of my brother, Tom, and the last of the nine spouses of the adult children of Wilson and Ieula Baird. I was asked to include this written copy of the eulogy I was privileged to give at Rowena's funeral.

Mrs. Rowena Edge Baird
August 8, 1924 — September 24, 2008

In the midst of our living, death, in its intrusive way, has once again come to dwell among us. So we gather to comfort one another and to put arms of love around one another.

In my brief years as a pastor (since 1986), I have conducted dozens of funerals and graveside services, and I have participated in dozens more. But today, I hardly know where to start because there are so many things I would like to say - things that could be said …things that should be said as we gather this morning to celebrate the life of Rowena Edge Baird - wife, mother, grandmother and now great grandmother to little Zoe.

Rowena was my sister-in-law . . . really, my precious sister. She was also Aunt Rowena to a long extended line of nieces and nephews. Numerous family and friends loved Rowena and gather with us today to celebrate her life - Rowena's beautiful Christian life - her open arms and open love and her living witness among us.

We gather also to celebrate eternal life - eternal life through our blessed Lord Jesus Christ, the One whom Rowena trusted and faithfully served as her Savior and Lord.

Both Rowena and I were teenaged brides. My big brother, Tom, thought I was foolish to marry so young. Then, he later married a precious girl, also still in her teens.

It was 1941 and war clouds were gathering.

So it turned out that Rowena and I went through World War II together. We were both still in our teens when the Japanese bombed Pearl Harbor, and President Roosevelt declared war on Dec 7, 1941.

A draft was started, and 1942 was a scary and bloody time for our generation.

If we were "The Greatest Generation," it was because we were perhaps the last generation where it was politically correct to openly talk about one's Christian faith.

By 1943, my brother, Tom, Rowena's husband, and Charles Shaw, my husband, were both serving abroad - Tom in Europe and Charles in the South Pacific.

Rowena lived with my mother who loved her like her own daughter . . . and Rowena loved and honored my mother like her own mother. At the time, Rowena was in a difficult pregnancy. She almost died in giving birth to their beautiful baby boy, Jack, while Tom was overseas.

It was a time when Rowena and I both learned - or tried to learn - how to pray. Down through the years, it was always good for me to know that Rowena Baird was praying for me ...and praying for you...all of you whom she knew.

Rowena continued to be a happy witnessing Christian, devoted to her husband and her son and later her daughter, Jane. She had a great sense of humor, was active in her church, including teaching Sunday school. Rowena was a Christian role model any of us would do well to emulate.

Rowena and Tom's Christian witness continued through some of the most difficult and heart breaking situations any of us could think to have to deal with. Jack, their precious son, died in an accident at age 22. Later, their grandson, Ray - the oldest son of Jane and her husband, Warren - died in a plane crash coming home from a mission trip to Venezuela.

Their faith in God sustained them and our Lord held them close in His arms in the midst of unspeakable sorrow.

As both Tom and Rowena told me, one does not "get over" the death of a child or grandchild, but somehow they had to learn - as we all try to learn - that God doesn't measure time in the same way we do. Death is a part of every life. We know that our children will die sooner or later. We always pray that it will be later. Psalm 90 tells us, "a thousand years are as a day and as a watch in the night."

I heard Christopher Reeve being interviewed, and he was asked what he had learned in the years since he was paralyzed. He replied that he had learned that "we are not our body."

Christopher may or may not have known it, but this is the Good News we celebrate today in the midst of our grief. We all know that our bodies, at best, are wearing out. Thank God we are not our bodies.

In fact, we are not a "body with a spirit" as much as we are a "spirit" in a temporary physical body.

Rowena seemed to know last Wednesday afternoon that her body had worn out, so she laid it aside. As Jane and I agreed yesterday: When Rowena took her last breath Wednesday afternoon, she was safe in the arms of Jesus and Tom was waiting for her at the Gate.

At death we come to the end of human knowledge, human power and human comfort. Human beings can go just so far along the path of life with another person. Thus, our precious Jane went as far as she could go with her dear mother on Wednesday; she finally had to let go of her mother's hand, knowing Rowena was safe in the hands of Jesus.

I am going to close by reading one of my poems that Rowena especially liked.

A few years before my husband died, we bought a cemetery lot —
sight unseen — in East View Cemetery in Conyers, where Charles'
parents and grandparents are buried.

Charles was still pastor of a busy church, and so it was some time
before we went down to see the cemetery lot we had bought. We
were there late one afternoon and remained as it began to get dark.
I noticed lights beginning to go on in homes near the cemetery
grounds. It seemed like a parable to me - like the remembrance of
parents leaving a light on until their children returned home at
night. So, I wrote these few simple lines:

The Light

My father always left a light for me
Against the nighttime shadows… lovingly

He left the doors unlocked…it opened wide
And I could safely find my way inside!

Beyond the grave…I see a light…I see
The lights of home…God left a light for me,

So I can walk on home…with faith…not fear
I see the Lights of Home…and God is near!

~Ruth Baird Shaw~

Regardless of what kind of shadows are falling around us today,
Rowena would not want us to walk in the shadows.

Lift up your hearts . . . there is light beyond the cemetery.

There is the Light of God … The light of the world.
There is resurrection. Thanks be to God!

Just a short time ago, in a daily e-mail from "Word-a-Day," a poet
and Nobel Laureate Rabindraneth Tagor was quoted, "Death is not

extinguishing the light; it is putting out the lamp because the dawn has come."

For Rowena, the dawn of a new day has come. Her race is run. Henceforth is laid up for her a crown.

As I close my part of this time of remembrance and celebration of the life of Rowena Baird, we praise God for this beautiful lady, rich in love and good works . . . friendly . . . always gracious and kind . . . a Christian lady.

Gratefully, but ever so reluctantly, we yield back...the gift of Rowena.

Happy Birthday to My Precious Daughter Debi on Nov. 14!

I am the mother of seven. Words are inadequate to tell how much each one fills my heart to overflowing with love. There are all kinds of stories to tell, as all of you who are parents know. Perhaps few are quite as dramatic as the one I tell today about Debi.

I'm holding Debi in this photo from 1952

Debi, now a wife and the mother of four sons and a daughter, is doing a great job on the staff of our church as the director of the church's day school.

This story is about the time we left our daughter, Deborah, at a service station near the Ohio River. Debi tells me when she and her husband, Gregg, and their family moved to Rome in 1988 and went to church at Trinity UMC, a woman who was introduced to her said, "Oh, you are the one they left at a service station in Ohio!"

Our son, Terrell, and his wife, Sheila, had been members at Trinity UMC for several years and had told this dramatic story to friends at the church.

My husband, Charles Shaw, had served as Trinity's pastor and we had lived in Trinity's parsonage for 6 years which were high school years for Terrell, Carol and Deborah. Both Terry and Debi are noted story tellers so my unvarnished account of the incident may not be as exciting as theirs.

When our five youngest children were small, we were on a camping trip vacation- traveling from our home in Ellijay, Georgia to Kentucky and Ohio. We stopped for gas at a service station in Louisville, Kentucky. The service station was within a few feet of the bridge that crosses the Ohio River.

All the children had been to the bathroom and were back in our nine-passenger station wagon. I was to learn later that Debi suddenly remembered she had left her hair barrette in the rest room. So she slipped out of the car to get it while I was feeding baby David in the front seat and while her siblings were getting settled in their places.

Charles came back from paying the bill and started the car, turning the few yards onto the long bridge that spans the Ohio River.

Carol, just two and a half years older than Debi, saw a huge ship on the Ohio River and said, "Look everybody! Look, Debi! Mama, where's Debi?"

I panicked. Charles panicked. We all panicked, quickly realizing we could not make a U-turn on the bridge. If there had been any physical way to

Debi petting our Chihuahua, Hercules, while her sister, Carol, looks on

turn around on that bridge, everyone who knew Charles Shaw knows he would have found it!

Charles pulled over as soon as we got off the bridge on the Ohio side and was turning our car around when much to our delight and relief the service station owner pulled in right behind us - bringing Debi to us.

Debi now tells the story to her children and to other children and adults in her own dramatic way. She tells that the man in the service station probably thought, 'These folks have been dropping off children all the way from Georgia, but they are not leaving one here!'"

Debi and Gregg and their 4 sons, daughter and
daughter-in-law in 2009

Whatever he thought, when Debi came finally out of the rest room to see us crossing the bridge, the service station owner put her in his truck and brought her to us.

The picture of that beautiful little face looking out that truck window is one that is still etched on my memory. I will never forget the joy and thanksgiving of seeing her little head in that truck and the kindness of the gas station owner.

Happy Birthday to My Precious Daughter Joan on Nov. 24!

Joan is the second of our seven children. She was born to my husband and me while I was still in my teens. We had a lot to learn. But no parents of any age could have welcomed a more beautiful baby into the world nor cherished a child more.

Words and/or pictures are inadequate to tell how much each of our children fills my heart to overflowing with love and how much Joan has a special place in my heart as she did in her Daddy's heart. She calls her blog, **Daddy's Roses**. There are all kinds of stories to tell about Joan as a child and as a beautiful and outstanding adult.

Joan was only a few months old in this photo

Joan was a rising senior in high school when we uprooted her from Griffin High School, a small city school where her friends, including a boyfriend, lived. We moved to Ellijay, a small mountain town in North Georgia. If you have ever had to move a teen away from friends, you know Joan was not a happy camper.

Ellijay was a town we had never heard of in 1958 when my husband, an ordained itinerant Elder in the Methodist Church, was sent to pastor a church there. The word, "itinerant" in the Methodist Church then, as now, means "traveling" and pastors then, even more than now, were ask to "travel" to any place where the Bishop and Cabinet thought they would best serve the overall church. Without much notice, but with commitment to Christ and the church, we were assigned to the church in Ellijay.

The annual North Georgia Conference moving day was a "fruit basket turn over" day. One pastor's family moved out of a Methodist parsonage and another moved in, sometimes just minutes apart. So with our moving van (actually a truck) following, we were finally on our way to a town we had never seen.

We had lived in Griffin four happy years so we had a week of sad good-byes and going away parties, along with packing and cleaning. Moving out of a parsonage and getting it ready for another family to move in immediately is work, work, and work!

Joan and Jim's grandchildren: Dow, Rachael, Brianne, Natalie, AnnaGrace and Ethan

So Charles and I were happy to finally be on our way. The younger children were excited about moving to the mountains and kept saying things like, "Mama, are those our mountains?" as we drove nearer and nearer to a place which did soon become "our" mountains and our home town.

Finally we got to the Ellijay city limits. Charles, in his own exuberant way, said, "The population of Ellijay has now increased by nine! " Joan, who had been very quiet, finally spoke, "It has probably doubled."

Joan and her husband, Jim Turrentine

But Joan adjusted well to her last year of high school there, was elected treasurer of her senior class and even had the fun of being on the Homecoming Court and a cheer leader for Gilmer High. She, along with all of us, made lifelong friends with some of the finest people this world ever produced.

Joan, now the wife of a United Methodist pastor knows more than she wanted to know about moving. She is also the happy Christian mother of a daughter and a son and now mother of a son-in-law and a daughter-in law and the fond and involved grandmother of six precious grandchildren.

Happy Birthday to My Precious Daughter Beth on Dec. 19!

I am the mother of seven. Each one has a very special place in my heart. There are all kinds of stories to tell about each one, as all of you who are parents know.

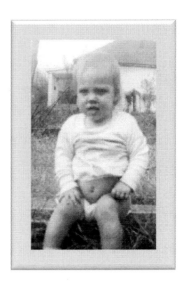

Beth is our baby girl. I know what it is like to be the baby in a family. People like to imply or say outright that the baby girl or boy in a family is a "spoiled brat." It was said about our youngest, our son David, and it was said about Beth, our youngest daughter. When I was a child, it was said about me as the youngest of 11. Not true! Well…perhaps a little?

Each one of our children also had a special place in their Daddy's heart and life. Beth's Daddy was a pastor and was told on the day of her birth he had plenty of time to go to church and get back to me at the hospital. However, Beth got in a hurry to make her appearance and came into the world at 12 noon on a Sunday,

Beth with her son, Joshua, and her daughter, Amanda

December 19, just as her father was pronouncing the benediction and hurrying out the church door to go back the few miles to the hospital.

Her Daddy's first words to me after visiting the nursery to see his fifth daughter was, "She is easily the most beautiful baby in the nursery, and I heard a man say, 'Look at that baby! One can tell she is a girl - look at those beautiful lips.'" Beth was and is feminine - all woman!

Beth and her younger brother were members of the UMC Youth choir in which she was a soloist with David at the keyboard. Her high school choral director predicted she would "go places" with her "big beautiful" voice for such a small girl. She's only a little over 5 feet tall.

One of the pictures I want to post wishing Beth a Happy Birthday is one of her giving a concert with her brother David at the piano. The event was at The Joyful Noise, a supper club in a suburb of Atlanta.

Beth singing at The Joyful Noise

Beth is also a wife, the mother of a son, a daughter, a daughter-in-law and a son-in- law and the happy grandmother of Emma.

Happy Birthday Dear Jesus on December 25!

Birthdays are special occasions in our family. When our children were young, the mood was always festive; and although the gifts were inexpensive, there was always a birthday gift and a home-made cake with candles. And singing! The honoree was awakened to the tune of "Happy birthday to you."

One Christmas, four year old David asked, "Are we going to sing 'Happy Birthday, Dear Jesus?'"

Happy Birthday, Dear Jesus

Happy birthday dear Jesus
Today with festive fare
We celebrate your birthday
With music in the air!
Cakes are baked and waiting
Candles light the tree.
Gifts are wrapped and ribboned
Is there no gift for Thee?
Jesus on Thy birthday morning
I kneel beside Thy crèche and see
Love incarnate - God's gift
And bring myself to Thee!

~Ruth Baird Shaw~

Charles and Ruth Shaw's Family

Children

Janice Dianne Shaw Crouse (married to Gilbert Crouse)
Lynda Joan Shaw Turrentine (married to James Turrentine)
Charles Terrell Shaw (married to Sheila Matthews Shaw)
Mary Carol Shaw Johnston (married to Ronald Johnston)
Deborah Ruth Shaw Lewis (married to Gregg Lewis)
Sharlyn Beth Shaw Roszel (married to Charles Roszel)
David Baird Shaw (married to Vicki Brown Shaw)

Grandchildren

Lyn Turrentine Davis
Charmaine Crouse Yoest
Gilbert Crouse, Jr.
Steven Turrentine
Larisa Johnston Hensiek
Joseph Johnston
Andrew Lewis
Joshua Hearn
Matthew Lewis
Amanda Hearn Sims
Brannon Shaw
Lisette Lewis
Jessica Shaw Rogers
Benjamin Lewis
Lillian Shaw
Jonathan Lewis
Catherine Shaw
Haley Shaw

Great Grandchildren

Rachael Turrentine
Hannah Yoest
Dow Turrentine
John Yoest
Lewis Crouse
Helena Yoest
Mark Crouse
Brianne Davis
AnnaGrace Turrentine
Natalie Davis
Sarah Yoest
Ethan Davis
Lily Hensiek
Sophie Hensiek
James Yoest
Emma Hearn
Evey Johnston
Alex Rogers

About The Author

Ruth Shaw holds a Masters of Divinity degree from Candler School of Theology, Emory University. She also earned a Bachelor's degree in Interdisciplinary Studies from the College of Arts and Sciences at Georgia State University and a Certificate in Gerontology for work in the field of aging.

As an elder in the United Methodist Church, North Georgia Conference, the Reverend Shaw served as pastor at Rico United Methodist Church in Palmetto, Grantville First United Methodist Church and East Point Avenue United Methodist Church in East Point.

After retiring to Rome in 1998, Ruth served on the staff at Trinity United Methodist Church for 4 years, as a short term interim pastor at Lyerly United Methodist Church for five months, at Oostanaula United Methodist Church for 13 months and with Livingston United Methodist for 12 months.

Mrs. Shaw is the author of **Recipes, Rhymes and Reflections, Life with Wings** and **The Chronicles of Ruth**. Ruth has read her poetry and spoken on the subject of aging often as a lay person to church and civic groups. After age 80, she continues to preach at every opportunity and often cooks for 25 to 50 family members and friends on special occasions.

Ruth Baird Shaw is the widow of the Reverend Charles C. Shaw who was an Elder and served in the North Georgia Conference of the United Methodist Church from 1954 until his death on December 3, 1986. He served as a student pastor in the Kentucky Methodist Conference from 1950 to 1954.